面向"十三五"职业教育精品规划教材

大学英语①

◎主编 项 莉

北京理工大学出版社
BEIJING INSTITUTE OF TECHNOLOGY PRESS

版权专有　侵权必究

图书在版编目（CIP）数据

大学英语.1/项莉主编.—北京：北京理工大学出版社，2018.6 重印
 ISBN 978-7-5682-4575-3

Ⅰ.①大…　Ⅱ.①项…　Ⅲ.①英语–高等学校–教材　Ⅳ.① H319.39

中国版本图书馆 CIP 数据核字（2017）第 196266 号

出版发行 / 北京理工大学出版社有限责任公司
社　　址 / 北京市海淀区中关村南大街 5 号
邮　　编 / 100081
电　　话 /（010）68914775（总编室）
　　　　　（010）82562903（教材售后服务热线）
　　　　　（010）68948351（其他图书服务热线）
网　　址 / http：//www.bitpress.com.cn
经　　销 / 全国各地新华书店
印　　刷 / 定州启航印刷有限公司
开　　本 / 787 毫米 × 1092 毫米　1/16
印　　张 / 11.25　　　　　　　　　　　　　　责任编辑 / 张荣君
字　　数 / 276 千字　　　　　　　　　　　　　文案编辑 / 张荣君
版　　次 / 2018 年 6 月第 1 版第 2 次印刷　　　　责任校对 / 周瑞红
定　　价 / 32.00 元　　　　　　　　　　　　　责任印制 / 边心超

图书出现印装质量问题，请拨打售后服务热线，本社负责调换

编写委员会

主　编： 项　莉
副主编： 左启利　孟宪兰
参　编：（按拼音首字母排列）
　　　　　关冬焕　姜晓坤　梁玉涛　吕艳双
　　　　　孙旭萍　王小彩　张　浩　张　红

前 言

《大学英语①》根据教育部颁发的《高职高专教育英语课程教学基本要求》编写，是高职高专普通英语课程的教学用书。

本套教材吸取了现行国内外同类教材的优点，以我国高职高专人才培养特点和教学改革的最新成果为依据，突出教学内容的实用性和针对性，将语言基础能力与实际涉外交际能力的培养有机结合，满足了21世纪全球化社会经济发展对高职高专人才的要求。《大学英语综合教程》共有两册，书中对各知识点的讲解翔实细致，不但在各单元呈现与时俱进的专题课文内容，还设置了形式多样的拓展习题，既有利于教师课上讲授，也便于学生自学。

具体来说，本套教材具有以下几个特点。

1. 注重提高综合素质，重点培养听说能力。本套教材根据高等教育英语教学内容和课程体系改革的要求，以听、说为重点，在每个单元专门开设听、说板块，把听、说、读、写、译的技能训练有机地结合起来。

2. 强调教学内容的整体性。本套教材将听、说内容与读、写内容相结合，将精读、泛读融为一体，使听、说、读、写、译五种技能的训练和培养围绕着同一主题展开，形成一个有机的整体。

3. 着眼于提高学生的职业技能和素质。本套教材根据高等教育英语教学的特点，提供与重点话题相关的实用训练，力求使学生通过切合实际的学习过程打下坚实的基础，在日常或涉外工作时能更加熟练地使用英语。

4. 选材广泛，注重"跨文化"知识的教学。本套教材注重选材内容的趣味性、信息性和实用性，注重语言的规范性和文体的多样性。为了更好地将文化内容与语言材料相融合，本套教材专门开辟板块介绍西方文化背景，使学生加深对所学内容的文化背景认识。

本书为《大学英语①》，共分为八个单元，每个单元包括七大板块，涵盖听、说、读、写、译各方面。

Preface

七大板块的主要内容如下。

第一部分是"Warm\up",主要是为学生学习新知识进行铺垫,要求学生围绕本课主题进行词汇联想并回答相关问题。

第二部分是"Speaking and Listening"。其中,Section A 是一段听力对话,要求学生进行跟读,旨在培养学生的听力和口语交际能力;Section B 是一段听力短文,要求学生在听短文的基础上填写空缺的单词,旨在提高学生听力的精准度。

第三部分是"Detailed Reading",要求学生对文章进行精读,课文后附有阅读理解练习题。其中,课文后的"Phrases and Expressions"部分所列的词组或短语均附有例句,便于学生掌握和运用。

第四部分是"Exercises",主要包括词义配对、选词填空和汉译英三种题型。其中,汉译英部分重点考查学生对词组、短语或固定搭配的运用。

第五部分是"Supplementary Reading",是扩展阅读部分,课文后附有阅读理解类问答题。扩展阅读部分主要培养考生精读和泛读的能力。

第六部分是"Grammar",主要讲解高职高专学生应掌握的语法知识。语法讲解后的练习题形式多样,难度适中。练习题在的编排上,力求与大学英语 A 级、B 级和四级考试的题型在最大程度上达到统一。

第七部分是"Writing",主要介绍日常应用文,如信件、贺卡等的写作,帮助学生通过范文学习和练笔掌握各类应用文的写作技巧。

在本套教材的编写过程中,编者参考、引用了一些文献资料和网站资源以及部分国内外专家学者的研究成果,在此谨向有关作者和为本套教材的出版付出辛勤劳动的编辑出版人员,以及帮助、支持本套教材编写的同仁、朋友致以诚挚的谢意。

由于编者水平有限,书中难免有疏漏之处,还请读者提出宝贵意见。

编 者

目 录
CONTENTS

Unit 1　College Life　/ 1
　　Part One　Warm-up　/ 1
　　Part Two　Speaking and Listening　/ 2
　　Part Three　Detailed Reading　/ 3
　　Part Four　Exercises　/ 6
　　Part Five　Supplementary Reading　/ 7
　　Part Six　Grammar　/ 9
　　Part Seven　Writing　/ 15
　　Culture Notes　/ 17

Unit 2　Books　/ 18
　　Part One　Warm-up　/ 18
　　Part Two　Speaking and Listening　/ 19
　　Part Three　Detailed Reading　/ 19
　　Part Four　Exercises　/ 23
　　Part Five　Supplementary Reading　/ 24
　　Part Six　Grammar　/ 26
　　Part Seven　Writing　/ 34
　　Culture Notes　/ 36

Unit 3　Generation　/ 37
　　Part One　Warm-up　/ 37
　　Part Two　Speaking and Listening　/ 38
　　Part Three　Detailed Reading　/ 38
　　Part Four　Exercises　/ 42
　　Part Five　Supplementary Reading　/ 43

　　Part Six　Grammar　/ 45
　　Part Seven　Writing　/ 51
　　Culture Notes　/ 53

Unit 4　Friendship　/ 54
　　Part One　Warm-up　/ 54
　　Part Two　Speaking and Listening　/ 55
　　Part Three　Detailed Reading　/ 55
　　Part Four　Exercises　/ 59
　　Part Five　Supplementary Reading　/ 60
　　Part Six　Grammar　/ 63
　　Part Seven　Writing　/ 67

Test Paper 1　/ 70

Unit 5　Romance　/ 78
　　Part One　Warm-up　/ 78
　　Part Two　Speaking and Listening　/ 79
　　Part Three　Detailed Reading　/ 80
　　Part Four　Exercises　/ 84
　　Part Five　Supplementary Reading　/ 85
　　Part Six　Grammar　/ 87
　　Part Seven　Writing　/ 94
　　Culture Notes　/ 95

Unit 6　Money　/ 96
　　Part One　Warm-up　/ 96
　　Part Two　Speaking and Listening　/ 97

Part Three   Detailed Reading   / 97
Part Four   Exercises   / 101
Part Five   Supplementary Reading   / 103
Part Six   Grammar   / 106
Part Seven   Writing   / 111

Unit 7   Internet   / 113
Part One   Warm-up   / 113
Part Two   Speaking and Listening   / 114
Part Three   Detailed Reading   / 115
Part Four   Exercises   / 119
Part Five   Supplementary Reading   / 120
Part Six   Grammar   / 123

Part Seven   Writing   / 131
Culture Notes   / 132

Unit 8   Entertainment   / 133
Part One   Warm-up   / 133
Part Two   Speaking and Listening   / 134
Part Three   Detailed Reading   / 134
Part Four   Exercises   / 138
Part Five   Supplementary Reading   / 139
Part Six   Grammar   / 142
Part Seven   Writing   / 147

Test Paper 2   / 149

Appendix   Glossary   / 159

Unit 1

College Life

 Part One   Warm-up

1. Think of terms related to college life and put them in the following box.

2. What are your expectations of your college life?
3. What are your plans for your college life?
4. What do you think are the most important aspects of college life?

Part Two Speaking and Listening

Section A Listen to the following conversation and then repeat.

Tom: Hi, Sandy.
Sandy: Hi, Tom.
Tom: How are you doing?
Sandy: Fine, thanks. How about you?
Tom: Good. Thanks. Do you know Tony? He's in your class.
Sandy: Certainly, in fact he was the first person I got to know in my class. I still remember the look on his face when he showed up late on the first day of school.
Tom: By the way, I am planning to take Computer Science this semester. Can you recommend (推荐) a professor?
Sandy: Sure. I'd recommend Doctor Williams. I heard that he is one of the best professors in our university.
Tom: Thanks a lot.

Section B Listen to the following short passage and fill in the missing words.

Good morning, everyone. I'd like to welcome you to Harvard University. I'm Alice Young and I work in the International Students' Office. I have some 1) _____ information for you. First, you must 2) _____ by August 30th. Pick up your ID card at our office. Then, you'll need to pick up a library card so that you can borrow books from the library. Show them your ID card in the library and they will do it for you. You may be thinking about the sports 3) _____ at our school. There's no 4) _____ for student use, but of course you'll have to show your ID card. Concerning the 5) _____ assistance, the university has its own health center, and all services are free for all students.

Unit 1

Part Three Detailed Reading

A research says that the present relationship between families and schools is not very harmonious. Some schools state that families often give children far more love and care which makes children self-centered. At the same time, families complain that schools make students nervous and arouse more worries to students.

Family education has its own advantages and disadvantages. Parents' words and actions can influence children's inner attitude towards the world. It is also very important for children to learn how to feel others' love and how to pay back in return. However, what family members can teach is quite limited. Children can only touch something inner but not many useful skills. Therefore, although family education is important for children's growth, it is far from enough for children to create a bright future.

Compared with family education, however, school education seems more necessary and useful. Firstly, students could acquire as much knowledge as possible of different fields. Schools have a lot of available resources in libraries and lectures which are able to provide enough information to students. Secondly, a school is like a society where different persons with different characters live together. Thus, students can greatly benefit from the environment and build up correct, positive and independent personalities. Thirdly, all kinds of organizations and activities help students a lot to learn how to communicate with different kinds of people and how to handle problems by themselves. But there are also some shortcomings, such as unreasonable teaching system and poorly-designed exams.

In short, both family education and school education play important roles in students' life. But neither of them is perfect. So families and schools should join hands tightly. In the hope of contributing to children's healthy growth and magnificent future, families and schools should make the most of each other's advantages and the least of each other's disadvantages.

New Words

harmonious	[hɑːˈməunɪəs]	adj.	existing together in harmony 和谐的
self-centered	[ˌselfˈsentəd]	adj.	interested only in oneself 以自我为中心的
complain	[kəmˈpleɪn]	v.	to express complaints, discontent, displeasure, or unhappiness 抱怨
arouse	[əˈraʊz]	v.	to call forth (emotions, feelings, and responses) 引起
advantage	[ədˈvɑːntɪdʒ]	n.	the quality of having a superior or more favorable position 好处
disadvantage	[ˌdɪsədˈvɑːntɪdʒ]	n.	the quality of having an inferior or less favorable position 不利
inner	[ˈɪnə(r)]	adj.	located or occurring within or closer to a center 内在的
attitude	[ˈætɪtjuːd]	n.	a complex mental state involving beliefs, feelings, values and dispositions to act in certain ways 态度
limited	[ˈlɪmɪtɪd]	adj.	small in range or scope 有限的
compare	[kəmˈpeə(r)]	v.	to examine and note the similarities or differences of two or more people or things 比较
knowledge	[ˈnɒlɪdʒ]	n.	facts, information, and skills acquired by a person through experience or education 知识
available	[əˈveɪləb(ə)l]	adj.	obtainable or accessible and ready for use or service 可用的；可得到的
information	[ˌɪnfə(r)ˈmeɪʃ(ə)n]	n.	a message received and understood 信息
society	[səˈsaɪəti]	n.	an extended social group having a distinctive cultural and economic organization 社会
character	[ˈkærɪktə(r)]	n.	the mental and moral qualities distinctive to an individual 性格
communicate	[kəˈmjuːnɪkeɪt]	v.	to transmit information 交流
handle	[ˈhænd(ə)l]	v.	to manage (a situation or problem) 处理
shortcoming	[ˈʃɔː(r)tˌkʌmɪŋ]	n.	a fault or failure to meet a certain standard, typically in a person's character, a plan, or a

			system 缺点
unreasonable	[ʌnˈriːz(ə)nəb(ə)l]	adj.	not guided by or based on good sense 不合理的
poorly-designed	[ˌpuəli-diˈzaind]	adj.	of something designed inadequately 设计不科学的
perfect	[ˈpəː(r)fikt]	adj.	being complete of its kind and without defect or blemish 完美的
contribute	[kənˈtribjuːt]	v.	to give something (especially money) in order to help achieve or provide something 有助于
magnificent	[mægˈnifis(ə)nt]	adj.	impressively beautiful, elaborate, or extravagant; striking 壮丽的，宏伟的

Phrases & Expressions

in short: in a word; to sum up 总之

例：In short, he is one of the most promising students I've ever known. 总之，他是我见过的最有前途的学生之一。

Comprehension of the Text

Choose the best answer for each of the following questions.

1. Family education can NOT _____.
   A. influence children's inner attitude towards the world
   B. teach children many useful skills
   C. teach children how to feel others' love
   D. teach children how to return others' love

2. In Para. 3, the disadvantages of school education include _____.
   A. unreasonable teaching system and poorly-designed exams
   B. making students self-centered
   C. providing little information to students
   D. making students nervous

3. Which of the following statements is NOT true according to the passage? _____
   A. Family education is far from enough for children to create a bright future.
   B. Schools have a lot of available resources to provide enough information to students.
   C. Children can learn how to communicate with different kinds of people in their family.
   D. Students could acquire as much knowledge as possible of different fields in schools.

4. What would be the best title for the passage? _____
   A. Family Education and School Education.

B. How to Create a Bright Future for Children.

C. What Is Education for?

D. The Advantage of School Education.

5. What is the main idea of this passage? _____

   A. The present relationship between families and schools is not very harmonious.

   B. Family education has more advantages than disadvantages.

   C. School education is better than family education.

   D. Family education and school education should join hands tightly for children to create a bright future.

 Part Four   Exercises

Task 1   Choose the definition from Column B that best matches each word or phrase in Column A.

A	B
1. character	a. to transmit information
2. perfect	b. not guided by or based on good sense
3. unreasonable	c. a message received and understood
4. handle	d. the mental and moral qualities distinctive to an individual
5. contribute	e. being complete of its kind and without defect or blemish
6. communicate	f. to manage (a situation or problem)
7. magnificent	g. existing together in harmony
8. information	h. to call forth (emotions, feelings, and responses)
9. harmonious	i. to give something (especially money) in order to help achieve or provide something
10. arouse	j. impressively beautiful, elaborate, or extravagant; striking

Task 2   Fill in the blanks with the words or expressions given below. Change the form where necessary.

handle	advantage	communicate	compare	harmonious
available	magnificent	arouse	information	complain

1. I _____ the copy with the original, but there was not much difference.

2. This was the only _____ room.

3. Her rich experience gave her an _____ over other applicants for the job.

4. He refused to allow his secretary to _____ confidential（机密的）letters.
5. We visited a _____ palace in the city.
6. Your _____ is inaccurate and your conclusion is therefore wrong.
7. Relations with our neighbors are very _____ at the moment.
8. The tourist _____ that the room was too dirty.
9. His sufferings _____ our sympathy（同情）.
10. We learn a language in order to _____ .

Task 3 Translate the following sentences into English, paying special attention to the underlined parts.

1. 他总是乐于助人。作为回报，大家都喜欢他。(in return)
2. 跟家庭教育相比，学校教育看起来更为必要和实用。(compare)
3. 她去跳舞，以增进健康。(build up)
4. 将这个与那个比较一下，你就会知道哪个比较好了。(compare)
5. 电脑在现代生活中起着重要的作用。(play a role in)

Part Five   Supplementary Reading

How Does One Choose a Major

With hundreds of majors and thousands of colleges and universities from which to choose, how does one begin to decide what and where to study? For some, the first decision is to choose a major.

Some have a passion for a subject. Some have an area in which they excelled in high school. Some have a career goal that will help them choose the major, for example, nursing, teaching, studio art, or engineering. But many students just don't know.

Most educators agree that in choosing a major, students should consider what they like to do, what their abilities are, and how they like to learn. Some of the best resources for helping choose a major come from colleges and universities themselves. A large number of institutions post on their Web sites a wealth of information and tools to help prospective and current students select majors. The most frequently cited advice includes:

Learn more about yourself. What are your academic strengths and weaknesses? What do you enjoy? What are your interests? What are your values? What are your immediate goals after graduating — getting a job or going to graduate school?

Take a personality or an interest assessment. If such assessment opportunities are not available in your secondary school or town, you can check at a U.S. Educational Advising/ Information Center in your home country.

Visit Web sites of university departments. Look at the majors offered. Analyze the courses offered and the degree requirements. Some college faculty members post their course requirement, a full description of the courses, online. The more you can learn about the types of courses and work required for a major, the better.

Once you are in the United States, go to departmental offices on campus. You can talk with staff, faculty, and students. Visit college career centers and look for reports that list jobs recent graduates have found, as well as the subject area in which the graduate majored.

After you enroll, try out different courses in different departments. Learn about the faculty members who teach the major courses and about what kind of students enroll.

If you find yourself in the wrong major, don't worry. Most students in U.S. colleges change their majors. Do not stay in a major you don't like or which is not challenging and stimulating.

Don't confuse a career choice with a major choice. Any major can prepare you for a number of different job possibilities. As the University of Washington states on its Web site, "A college education helps prepare you for the job market but doesn't limit you to a specific career."

(This text is adapted from http://www.america.gov/st/educ-english/2008/April/20080518234235SrenoD0.9282038.html, 2011-12-19.)

New Words

passion	[ˈpæʃən]	n.	strong feeling or emotion 激情，热情
excel	[ikˈsel]	v.	to distinguish oneself 超过，优于
career	[kəˈriə]	n.	job 职业，事业
prospective	[prəˈspektiv]	adj.	related to the future 未来的，预期的
current	[ˈkʌrənt]	adj.	belonging to the present time 现在的，当前的
assessment	[əˈsesmənt]	n.	the act of judging or assessing 估计，评估
faculty	[ˈfækəlti]	n.	the body of teachers at a school 全体教员
challenge	[ˈtʃælindʒ]	v.	to issue a challenge to 向……挑战
stimulate	[ˈstimjuleit]	v.	to stir somebody's feelings, emotions, or peace 激励,鼓舞

Phrases & Expressions

a wealth of：lots of 很多的，大量的

例：There's a wealth of books in the library. 这个图书馆藏书丰富。

Comprehension of the Text

Answer the following questions according to the text.

1. What should students consider when they choose a major?
2. What can students do if they choose a wrong major?
3. What is the difference between a career choice and a major choice?

Part Six Grammar

名词（Nouns）

一、名词概说

名词是表示人、动物、事物、地方、状态、品质或动作的名称的一类词。它可以表示具体的东西，也可以表示抽象的东西。

名词可以分为专有名词（Proper Nouns）和普通名词（Common Nouns）。专有名词表示某个（些）人、地方、机构等专有的名称，如 New York, England 等。普通名词表示一类人、东西或是一个抽象概念的名称，如 desk, happiness 等。普通名词又可分为下面四类：

(1) 个体名词：表示某类人或东西中的个体，如 man。
(2) 集体名词：表示若干个个体组成的集合体，如 family。
(3) 物质名词：表示无法分为个体的实物，如 water。
(4) 抽象名词：表示动作、状态、品质、感情等抽象概念，如 beauty。

个体名词和集体名词可以用数目来计算，称为可数名词；物质名词和抽象名词一般无法用数目计算，称为不可数名词。名词的分类可用表 1–1 表示。

表 1–1　名词的分类

名词	专有名词		
	普通名词	物质名词	不可数名词
		抽象名词	
		集体名词	可数名词
		个体名词	

二、名词复数常见的规则变化形式

名词复数常见的规则变化形式如表 1–2 所示。

表 1–2　名词复数常见的规则变化形式

情况	构成方法	读音	例词
一般情况	加 -s	清辅音后读 /s/	cap—caps
		浊辅音和元音后读 /z/	leg—legs / car—cars
以 s, sh, ch, x 等结尾	加 -es	读 /iz/	bus—buses / watch—watches
以 ce, se, ze 等结尾	加 -s	读 /iz/	license—licenses
以"辅音字母+y"结尾	变 y 为 i 再加 es	读 /z/	baby—babies

三、名词复数的其他规则变化形式

(1) 以 y 结尾的专有名词，或"元音字母+y"结尾的名词，变复数时直接加 s。例如：

two Marys　　　　　　　　　the Henrys
donkey—donkeys　　　　　　holiday—holidays

(2) 以 o 结尾的名词变复数时有以下几种变化形式。

① 加 s，例如：

photo—photos　　　　　　　piano—pianos
radio—radios　　　　　　　 zoo—zoos

② 加 es，例如：

potato—potatoes　　　　　　tomato—tomatoes

③ 上述①和②两种方法均可，例如：

zero—zeros / zeroes

（3）以 f 或 fe 结尾的名词变复数时有下列几种变化形式。

①加 s，例如：

belief—beliefs   roof—roofs
safe—safes   gulf—gulfs

②去 f, fe 加 ves，例如：

half—halves   knife—knives
leaf—leaves   wolf—wolves
wife—wives   life—lives
thief—thieves

③上述①和②两种方法均可，例如：

handkerchief—handkerchiefs / handkerchieves

四、名词复数的不规则变化形式

（1）名词形式的不规则变化，例如：

child—children   foot—feet   tooth—teeth
mouse—mice   man—men   woman—women

注意：由一个词加 man 或 woman 构成的合成词，其复数形式也是 -men 和 -women，例如 an Englishman, two Englishmen。但 German 不是合成词，故其复数形式为 Germans；Hoffman 是姓，其复数是 the Hoffmans。

（2）单复数同形，类似的词有：deer, sheep, fish, Chinese, Japanese, li, jin, yuan, mu 等，例如：two li, three mu, four jin。但除人民币的元、角、分外，美元、英镑、法郎等都有复数形式，例如：a dollar, two dollars；a meter, two meters。

（3）集体名词，以单数形式出现，但实为复数。例如，people, police, cattle 等本身就是复数，不能说 a people, a police, a cattle。但可以说 a person, a policeman, a head of cattle。the English, the British, the French, the Chinese, the Japanese, the Swiss 等名词，表示国民总称时，作复数用，例如：

The Chinese are industrious and brave. 中国人民是勤劳勇敢的。

（4）以 s 结尾，仍为单数的名词，例如：

①maths, politics, physics 等学科名词，一般是不可数名词，为单数。

②news 为不可数名词。

③the United States, the United Nations 应视为单数。例如：

The United Nations was organized in 1945. 联合国是 1945 年组建起来的。

④以复数形式出现的书名、剧名、报纸、杂志名，也可视为单数。例如：

"The Arabian Nights" is a very interesting storybook.

《一千零一夜》是一本非常有趣的故事书。

（5）表示由两部分构成的东西，如 glasses（眼镜），trousers, clothes 等，若表达具体数目，要借助数量词 pair（对，双），suit（套）等。例如：a pair of glasses, two pairs of trousers。

（6）另外，还有一些名词，其复数形式有时可以表示特别意思，例如：goods 意为 "货物"，waters 意为"水域"，fishes 意为"（各种）鱼"。

五、不可数名词量的表示

1. 物质名词

（1）当物质名词转化为个体名词时为可数。例如：

Cake is a kind of food. 蛋糕是一种食物。（不可数）

These cakes are sweet. 这些蛋糕是甜的。（可数）

（2）当物质名词表示该物质的种类时为可数。例如：

This factory produces steel. 这个工厂生产钢。（不可数）

We need various steels. 我们需要各种钢。（可数）

（3）当物质名词表示份数时为可数。例如：

Our country is famous for tea. 我国因茶叶而闻名。（不可数）

Two teas, please. 请来两杯茶。（可数）

2. 抽象名词

抽象名词表示具体的事例时也为可数。例如：

four freedoms 四大自由　　the four modernizations 四个现代化

物质名词和抽象名词可以借助单位词表示一定的数量，例如：

a glass of water 一杯水　　　a piece of advice 一则建议

六、定语名词的复数

名词作定语一般用单数，但也有以下例外。

（1）用复数作定语。例如：

sports meeting 运动会　　talks table 谈判桌　　the foreign languages department 外语系

（2）man, woman, gentleman 等作定语时，其单复数以所修饰的名词的单复数而定。例如：

men workers 男工人　　women doctors 女医生　　gentlemen officials 男性官员

（3）有些以 s 结尾的名词，作定语时，s 保留。例如：

goods train 货车　　　　　　arms produce 武器生产

customs papers 报关单　　　clothes brush 衣刷

（4）"数词+名词"作定语时，这个名词一般保留单数形式。例如：

two-dozen eggs 两打鸡蛋　　a ten-mile walk 十英里路

two-hundred trees 两百棵树　　a five-year plan 一个五年计划

七、表示不同国籍的人的名词的单复数

表示不同国籍的人的名词的单复数如表 1-3 所示。

表 1-3　表示不同国籍的人的名词的单复数

国籍	总称（谓语用复数）	单数	复数
中国人	the Chinese	a Chinese	two Chinese
瑞士人	the Swiss	a Swiss	two Swiss
澳大利亚人	the Australians	an Australian	two Australians
俄国人	the Russians	a Russian	two Russians
意大利人	the Italians	an Italian	two Italians

续表

国籍	总称（谓语用复数）	单数	复数
希腊人	the Greek	a Greek	two Greeks
法国人	the French	a Frenchman	two Frenchmen
日本人	the Japanese	a Japanese	two Japanese
美国人	the Americans	an American	two Americans
印度人	the Indians	an Indian	two Indians
加拿大人	the Canadians	a Canadian	two Canadians
德国人	the Germans	a German	two Germans
英国人	the English	an Englishman	two Englishmen
瑞典人	the Swedish	a Swede	two Swedes

八、名词的格

英语中有些名词可以加's 来表示所有关系，带这种词尾的名词形式称为该名词的所有格，如：a teacher's book。名词所有格的变化规则如下：

（1）单数名词词尾加's，复数名词词尾若没有 s，也要加's。例如：
the boy's bag 男孩的书包　　men's room 男厕所

（2）若名词已有复数词尾-s，只加'。例如：
the workers' struggle 工人的斗争

（3）凡不能加's 的名词，都可以用"名词+of+名词"的结构来表示所有关系。例如：
the title of the song 那首歌的名字

（4）在表示店铺或教堂的名字或某人的家时，名词所有格的后面常常不出现它所修饰的名词，如：
the barber's 理发店

（5）如果两个名词并列，并且分别有's，则表示"分别有"；只有一个's，则表示"共有"。例如：
John's and Mary's rooms（两间屋子）——John and Mary's room（一间屋子）

（6）复合名词或短语，'s 加在最后一个词的词尾。例如：
a month or two's absence（一两个月不在）

练　习

I. 选择题。

1. These tables are made of ＿＿＿＿.
   A. wood　　　B. woods　　　C. wooden　　　D. some woods

2. Mother went to her doctor for ＿＿＿＿ about her heart trouble.
   A. an advice　　B. advice　　C. advices　　D. the advices

3. He gained his ＿＿＿＿ by printing ＿＿＿＿ of famous writers.

    A. wealth; work   B. wealths; works

    C. wealths; work   D. wealth; works

4. Dr. Smith is going to pull out one of my _____.

    A. teeth   B. tooth   C. teeths   D. toothes

5. _____ on trees turn green in spring.

    A. Leaf   B. Leafs   C. Leave   D. Leaves

6. Miss Smith is a friend of _____.

    A. Mary's mother's   B. Mary's mother

    C. Mother's of Mary   D. Mary mother's

7. If this dictionary is not yours, _____ can it be?

    A. what else   B. who else   C. which else's   D. who else's

8. — I wonder whose bicycle it is.

    — It might be my _____.

    A. neighbour's   B. dear neighbour

    C. neighbour   D. neighbours

9. He dropped the _____ and broke it.

    A. cup of coffee   B. coffee's cup   C. cup for coffee   D. coffee cup

10. The village is far away from here indeed. It's _____ walk.

    A. a four hour   B. a four hour's   C. a four-hours   D. a four hours'

II. 将括号内的动词变成适当的形式填空。

1. English _____ (be) an important subject taught in the middle school.

2. Professor Li with his pupils _____ (keep) on the running exercise every morning.

3. Today's news _____ (be) quite surprising.

4. A large number of Japanese _____ (visit) China this year.

5. "The Selected Plays" _____ (be) among Lao She's main works.

6. Not only the students but also Mr. Wang _____ (join) in the basketball match.

7. The police _____ (find) the separated relation of Comrade Zhou's.

8. I think that physics _____ (be) more difficult than chemistry.

9. The pronunciation of English words _____ (be) not easy.

10. The pair of trousers _____ (be) too long for me.

III. 翻译下列句子，注意名词所有格表达的意思。

1. Zhou's and Li's bikes are now being repaired.

2. Zhou, Li and Wang's bike is now under repair.

3. When Dora and Jack's father lost his job, their living expenses had to be cut to the bone.

4. Your words carry more weight than anybody else's.

5. Alfred accepted the invitation without a moment's hesitation.
6. This article was carried in yesterday's *The People's Daily*.
7. He held the picture at an arm's length.
8. The two accounts of the accident do not agree.
9. There is a picture of Tom on the wall.
10. There is a picture of Tom's on the wall.

Part Seven   Writing

Registration Forms

Directions: In this part, you are going to learn how to fill in a *Registration Form* and then try your hand.

1. Read the following sample.

Registration Form of International Students

Full Name in English as in the Passport:		**David Robert Anderson**		
Given Name	**David**	Surname	**Anderson**	photo
Nationality	**American**	Passport No.	**FS200003864**	
Sex	**Male**	Date of Birth	**1985-05-23**	
Marital Status	**Single**	Place of Birth	**Atlanta**	
Religion	**None**	Email	**David85523@hotmail.com**	
Home Address		**323 Peachtree Street, NE Suite 1400, Atlanta**		
Highest Academic Degree Obtained		**A Bachelor of Arts Degree from University of Atlanta**		
Duration of Study		**From Sept. 2007 to June 2010**		
Chinese Proficiency:	**Good**			
Special Skills or Hobbies:	**Computer and Surfing the Internet**			
Financial Sponsor's Name:		**Mr. & Ms. Anderson**		
Address	**323 Peachtree Street, NE Suite 1400, Atlanta**		Tel	**404-656-3235**
Relationship with the Applicant:		**Parents and Son**		
Signature **David**			Date	**2010-09-15**

2. Exercise: Fill in the following Student Registration Form.

Student Registration Form

Department：   Student ID No.：

Name		Sex		Nationality		Photo
Date of Birth		Marital Status		Place of Birth		
Health		ID Card No.				
Mobile Phone		Email Address				
Home Address				Zip Code		
Name of Last School						
Special Skills or Hobbies						
English Proficiency						
Father's Name			Phone No.			
Mother's Name			Phone No.			

Signature：   Date：

Data Bank

full name 全名
surname 姓
nationality 国籍
DOB (Date of Birth) 出生日期
single 未婚
divorced 离婚
Christian 基督教徒
Islam 伊斯兰教徒
none 无；不会
excellent 很好
proficiency 熟练程度
poor 较差
hobby 爱好

given name 教名，名字
student ID number 学生证号
gender 性别
marital status 婚姻状况
married 已婚
religion 宗教信仰
Catholic 天主教徒
Buddhist 佛教徒
health 健康状况
fair 一般
good 良好
skill 技能

Tips

在实际生活中，国外的许多表格里都有多项的选择情况，你可以在选定的情况处打钩。

在 Nationality（国籍）一栏，中国籍学生应填 Chinese。而在 Country of Birth（出生地）一栏，可理解为填表者出生时所在的国家，中国学生应该填 China。

另外，在英语中，短语 fill in 和 fill out 在用于表达"填表格"的时候，意思相同，都是"填写"的意思。在日期写法上，英语有多种表达方式。比如，英国写法为"日/月/年"，美国则为"月/日/年"。如 2010 年 9 月 2 日：2nd Sept., 2010（英），Sept. 2nd, 2010（美）。填表格时，日期可全部用数字表达，但英美也有差别，分别为：02/09/2010（英），即"日/月/年"的填法；09/02/2010（美），即"月/日/年"的填法。当然，也有在中国人看来非常简单明了的填法：2010-09-02。

Culture Notes

The Ivy League

The eight universities known as Ivy League schools are Brown University, Columbia University, Cornell University, Dartmouth College, Harvard University, University of Pennsylvania, Princeton University, and Yale University. The idea dates back to October, 1933 when Stanley Woodward, a sports writer for the *New York Herald Tribune*, used the phrase "ivy colleges" to describe these schools, which had common sports programs. Since the colleges were among the first established in the United States, most have distinguished and historic campuses featuring old, ivy-covered buildings; their league, and the member colleges, became known as the Ivy League.

February, 1954 is the accepted founding date of the Ivy League, but athletic competition between all eight schools did not formally begin until the 1956-1957 season when the presidents of the universities adopted a round-robin（循环赛）schedule for football. The phrase is no longer limited to athletics, and now represents an educational philosophy inherent to the nation's oldest schools.

All eight schools of "Ivy League" are among the top schools in the United States; they are the most historic and famous universities in the United States. The names of the schools and the name "Ivy League" continue to remind people of the image of excellence in American higher education.

Unit 2

Books

Part One   Warm-up

1. Can you list some books you have read? Put them in the following box.

2. Do you enjoy reading books? Why or why not?
3. If you have the time, which book do you want to read most?
4. What is your favorite book? Why do you like it?

Unit 2

Part Two Speaking and Listening

Section A Listen to the following conversation and then repeat.

Tom: Whose book is this?
Sandy: It's mine. Why do you ask?
Tom: Could I borrow it? I've been waiting to read it.
Sandy: Be my guest, but I warn you that it's not as good as they say.
Tom: What's the matter with it?
Sandy: Well, the plot is highly complicated.
Tom: That's strange. I've read three of his books and thought they were all well done.
Sandy: I've been a fan of him for a long time too, but he really disappointed me on this one!
Tom: What did the reviews say?
Sandy: They were mixed — some good, some bad. My review, bad!

Section B Listen to the following short passage and fill in the missing words.

　　The famous American writer Mark Twain once said: "The man who doesn't read good books has no 1) _____ over the man who can't read them." If you don't read, you are missing out on a great way of learning as well as a wonderful way of 2) _____ your life. Books can instruct, 3) _____, entertain, motivate and inspire. This is a simple and relatively 4) _____ method of growing up as a person. Drawing on the 5) _____ of the ages, books cover every subject you can imagine. So pick up a good book and read!

Part Three Detailed Reading

What Is the Holy Grail

The novel *The Da Vinci Code* is a very good suspense thriller. Author Dan Brown must either play or at least be aware of computer games: the plot has a computer game feel to it. The characters get into a situation of danger and must help themselves by solving a series of puzzles, with one puzzle's solution leading to another puzzle, which also requires a solution.

There are two characters, Robert Landon and Sophie Neveu — Robert an expert on religious symbology and a Harvard professor, and Sophie a cryptologist and Parisian police agent. Both have skill sets, not by accident, which allow for great success at solving puzzles — at least the type of puzzles presented here.

The opening chapter is fascinating. Jacques Sauniere, the director of the Louvre museum, is shot in the stomach by a monk named Silas and left to bleed slowly to death. Jacques Sauniere is, as chance and the author would have it, the grandfather of Sophie Neveu.

The time it takes Jacques to die is time enough for him to set up the first of the puzzles to be solved. His body is found lying on the floor, arms and legs spread, with writings (written by Jacques in his own blood) which are meant to be secret coded messages to his granddaughter, Sophie. Robert Landon is drawn into this murder as the inspector on the case, Bezu Faches, believes he is the killer. Sophie, knowing Robert is innocent, helps him escape from the Musee du Louvre, and the chase (and puzzle solving) is on.

The plot turns are suspenseful, the mysteries and their solutions clever, even creative in some cases. The plot here centers on an intellectual belief that Jesus (yes, the Christian Jesus) had a love affair and/or was married to Mary Magdalene, who was in fact pregnant with Jesus's child at the time of the crucifixion — a fact supposedly known by the Church and covered up. The "thing" everyone is being chased and killed for, is the secret of the location of the holy grail, a location known to many who belonged to a secret society throughout history, including Leonardo Da Vinci. No, the holy grail is not, under this theory, the cup Jesus drank wine from during the Last Supper, but rather a metaphor for Mary Magdalene. She is the "cup" that held Jesus's child: she is the true holy grail.

If you are interested in the source of the Mona Lisa's smile, or the fact that one of the figures in Da Vinci's "Last Supper" is a woman, read the book *The Da Vinci Code*!

(This text is adapted from a book review on the website http://www.curledup.com/davinci.htm, 2012-01-19.)

Unit 2

New Words

suspense	[səˈspens]	n.	eagerness about what is going to happen 悬疑，焦虑，悬念
thriller	[ˈθrilə]	n.	a suspenseful adventure story 惊险小说
plot	[plɔt]	n.	the story that is told in a novel, play, movie etc. 故事情节
puzzle	[ˈpʌzl]	n.	question that is difficult to understand or answer 难题，谜一样的事物
		v.	to make sb. think hard, perplex 使困惑
expert	[ˈekspəːt]	n.	a person with special knowledge or ability who performs skillfully 专家，能手
symbology	[simˈbɔlədʒi]	n.	the study or the use of symbols or symbolism 符号学
cryptologist	[kripˈtɔlədʒist]	n.	the person who studies the science of analysing or deciphering codes 密码学家
agent	[ˈeidʒənt]	n.	a representative who acts on behalf of other persons or organizations; a person who works for a government or police department, especially in order to get secret information about another country or organization 代理人；特工
present	[priˈzent]	v.	to show or demonstrate something to an interested audience 展示，展现
fascinate	[ˈfæsineit]	v.	to cause to be interested or curious 使着迷
bleed	[bliːd]	v.	to lose blood from one's body 流血
spread	[spred]	v.	to open from a closed or folded state 展开
code	[kəud]	v.	to convert ordinary language into code 写成密码或代码
murder	[ˈməːdə]	n.	unlawful killing of a human being 谋杀
case	[keis]	n.	a problem requiring investigation 案件
innocent	[ˈinəsnt]	adj.	free from evil or guilt 无罪的
intellectual	[ˌintiˈlektʃuəl]	adj.	of or relating to the intellect 智力的
pregnant	[ˈpregnənt]	adj.	carrying offspring within the body or being about to produce new life 怀孕的
crucifixion	[ˌkruːsiˈfikʃən]	n.	the death of Jesus on the cross 耶稣被钉死在十字架上
holy	[ˈhəuli]	adj.	associated with a divine power 神圣的，圣洁的
grail	[greil]	n.	(通常作 the Holy Grail) plate or cup used by Jesus 圣杯
metaphor	[ˈmetəfə]	n.	use of a word or phrase to indicate something different 隐喻

Phrases & Expressions

1. **be aware of**: to realize 意识到，知道，清楚

   例：Mary has been aware of having done something wrong. 玛丽已经意识到自己做错了事情。

2. **by accident**: by chance 偶然，碰巧

   例：I only found it by accident. 我只是碰巧找到的。

3. **center on**: to focus on 以……为中心，以……为主题

   例：The topic centers on the crisis in these two countries. 话题以那两个国家的危机为中心展开。

Comprehension of the Text

Choose the best answer for each of the following questions.

1. Which of the following is NOT true according to the text? _____
   A. *The Da Vinci Code* is a very good novel.
   B. Author Dan Brown must like playing computer games.
   C. The characters face danger and have to help themselves.
   D. There are a lot of puzzles in the novel which require solutions.

2. Which of the following is NOT true about Robert Landon? _____
   A. He is an expert on religious symbology.
   B. He is a Harvard professor who is good at symbols.
   C. He is believed by all to be the killer of Jacques Sauniere.
   D. He is drawn into the murder case.

3. Which of the following is NOT true about the director of the Louvre museum? _____
   A. He is shot dead in the stomach by a monk.
   B. He is left to bleed slowly to death.
   C. He is found lying on his stomach on the floor.
   D. He is the grandfather of Sophie Neveu.

4. What is the Holy Grail according to the novel? _____
   A. The cup Jesus drank wine from during the Last Supper.
   B. Mary Magdalene.
   C. Mona Lisa.
   D. A woman in Da Vinci's "Last Supper".

5. Which of the following adjectives can NOT be used to describe the novel? _____
   A. Fascinating.   B. Suspenseful.
   C. Mysterious.   D. Metaphorical.

Unit 2

Part Four   Exercises

Task 1   Choose the definition from Column B that best matches each word in Column A.

A	B
1. fascinate	a. a problem requiring investigation
2. puzzle	b. unlawful killing of a human being
3. present	c. use of a word or phrase to indicate something different
4. case	d. to lose blood from one's body
5. innocent	e. to cause to be interested or curious
6. metaphor	f. a suspenseful adventure story or play
7. bleed	g. free from evil or guilt
8. plot	h. to show or demonstrate something to an interested audience
9. thriller	i. the story that is told in a novel, play, movie etc.
10. murder	j. question that is difficult to understand or answer

Task 2   Fill in the blanks with the words or expressions given below. Change the form where necessary.

| agent | fascinate | case | innocent | plot |
| intellectual | puzzle | present | spread | expert |

1. The sudden fall in the value of the dollar has _____ financial experts.
2. Since there was no one else in the compartment (车厢), I was able to _____ myself.
3. According to _____ opinions, they gave up the experiment on the animal immediately.
4. A wonderful opportunity suddenly _____ itself.
5. The children were _____ by the toys in the window.
6. He was charged with murder but found _____ later.
7. FBI is on the lookout for the _____ these days for he behaved rather strange.
8. The argument was too _____ for me; I couldn't follow a word of it.
9. The _____ of the novel is well planned that I can not put it down.
10. The police was investigating the murder _____ .

Task 3   Translate the following sentences into English, paying special attention to the underlined parts.

1. 我很<u>清楚</u>工作职位非常少。(be aware)

23

2. 她的回答把我弄糊涂了。(puzzle)
3. 我想去外面伸展一下四肢。(spread oneself)
4. 这一谋杀案将在下星期审理。(murder case)
5. 他声称他是无罪的。(innocent)

Part Five　Supplementary Reading

How to Read Efficiently

Efficient reading helps you to understand the writer's message without spending too much time in the process. It also gives you a clear purpose in mind so that you only read material that is relevant. When you're reading, remember that good reading strategies go hand-in-hand with good note-taking skills.

Efficient reading starts with choosing a strategy to suit the kind of text you have to read. Your purposes in reading might include: gathering information for an essay; learning about a particular topic or understanding a particular theory; preparing for an exam.

In all of these cases, the nature of the text will help you decide how to read. The strategies for reading a textbook, for example, are different from those used when reading journal articles. Here three types of books are discussed.

Academic texts: Academic texts are relatively formal in structure and style. They might be textbooks or just straightforward texts. To increase the amount of information that you can extract from a single reading of an academic text, you need to use efficient academic reading strategies. You can read the introduction to search for the thesis point or main argument and you can verify the overview provided by the contents page. Or you can scan by topic sentences, i. e. the sentence which makes the point of the paragraph and which is usually the first sentence of the paragraph.

Standard texts: When reading a standard textbook, such as a general text in nursing, information can be gathered by using a variety of strategies. You can pay special attention to the overall structure of the textbook in terms of the following three aspects: the subdivision of the book into chapters; the subdivision of chapters into sections; and the subdivision of sections into subsections. It can also be extracted quickly at the level of subsections. You can simply note how topic sentences are used. They are quite useful in introducing the main focus of a paragraph and presenting an argument or an overall outline of ideas.

Journal articles: Journal articles usually have a quite rigid structure. This is determined by the kind of journal and by the type of research being reported; this makes extracting information from them sometimes easier than from less rigid text types. The reporting of research will mostly follow the format of abstract, introduction, methods, results, discussion, and conclusion.

New Words

efficient	[iˈfiʃənt]	adj.	being effective without wasting time or effort 效率高的，胜任的
relevant	[ˈrelivənt]	adj.	having a connection with the subject at issue 相关的，切题的
strategy	[ˈstrætidʒi]	n.	skillful planning in general 战略，策略
journal	[ˈdʒəːnl]	n.	a newspaper or magazine that deals with a particular subject of profession; a daily written record of experiences; diary 杂志，期刊，报纸，日报，日记
straightforward	[streitˈfɔːwəd]	adj.	frank 坦率的，直接的
extract	[iksˈtrækt]	v.	to remove (used in an abstract sense) 选取，摘录
thesis	[ˈθiːsis]	n.	a statement as a premise in an argument 论题，主题
argument	[ˈɑːgjumənt]	n.	a fact or assertion offered as evidence that something is true 论据
verify	[ˈverifai]	v.	to make sure that a factor or an argument is true 查证，证实
overview	[ˈəuvəˌvjuː]	n.	a general summary of a subject 概况，总结
overall	[ˌəuvəˈrɔːl]	adj.	including everything 全部的，全体的，一切在内的
aspect	[ˈæspekt]	n.	a distinct feature or element in a problem 方面
subdivision	[ˈsʌbdiˌviʒən]	n.	an area composed of subdivided lots 细分，再分的部分
subsection	[ˈsʌbˌsekʃən]	n.	a section of a section 小单位，细分
outline	[ˈautlain]	n.	a summary of the main points of an argument or theory 大纲，概要
rigid	[ˈridʒid]	adj.	very strict and difficult to change 刻板的，严格的
format	[ˈfɔːmæt]	n.	the general appearance of a publication 格式
abstract	[ˈæbstrækt]	n.	a short written statement containing the most important ideas in a speech, article etc. 摘要

Phrases & Expressions

pay attention to：to heed 注意，留意
例： He breezed in without paying attention to anyone. 他信步走了进来，对谁也不加注意。

Comprehension of the Text

Answer the following questions according to the text.

1. What are the purposes of the passage?
2. How many types of books are mentioned in the passage? What are they?
3. How can you get information from an academic book?

 Part Six Grammar

代词（Pronouns）（一）

一、代词概说

代词是用于代替名词的词类。大多数代词具有名词和形容词的功能。英语中的代词，按其意义、特征及在句中的作用分为：人称代词、物主代词、指示代词、反身代词、相互代词、不定代词、疑问代词和关系代词八种。

1. 人称代词

人称代词是表示"我""你""他""她""它""我们""你们""他们""她们""它们"的词。人称代词有人称、数和格的变化，见表2-1。

表2-1 人称代词人称、数和格的变化

数	单数		复数	
格	主格	宾格	主格	宾格
第一人称	I	me	we	us
第二人称	you	you	you	you
第三人称	he	him	they	them
	she	her	they	them
	it	it	they	them

例如：

He is my boss. 他是我的老板。

It's me. 是我。

2. 物主代词

物主代词是表示所有关系的代词，也可以叫代词所有格。物主代词分为形容词性物主代词和名词性物主代词两种，其人称和数的变化见表 2-2。

表 2-2　物主代词人称和数的变化

数	单数			复数		
人称	第一人称	第二人称	第三人称	第一人称	第二人称	第三人称
形容词性物主代词	my	your	his/her/its	our	your	their
名词性物主代词	mine	yours	his/hers/its	ours	yours	theirs

例如：

The boy likes his toy car. 这个男孩喜欢他的玩具小汽车。

Our house is here, and theirs is there. 我们的房子在这儿，他们的在那儿。

3. 指示代词

指示代词是表示"那个""这个""这些""那些"等指示概念的代词。指示代词有 this，that，these，those 等。例如：

That is an interesting story. 那是个有意思的故事。

4. 反身代词

表示"我自己""你自己""他自己""我们自己""你们自己"和"他们自己"等的代词，叫做反身代词，也称为"自身代词"。例如：

She was talking to herself. 她自言自语。

5. 相互代词

表示相互关系的代词叫相互代词，有 each other 和 one another 两组，但在运用中，这两组词没什么大的区别。例如：

They help each other. 他们相互帮助。

6. 不定代词

不指明代替任何特定名词的代词叫做不定代词。常见的不定代词有 all，both，each，every 等，以及含有 some-，any-，no-等的合成代词，如 anybody, something, no one。这些不定代词大都可以代替名词和形容词，在句中作主语、宾语、表语和定语，但 none 和由 some-，any-，no-等构成的复合不定代词只能作主语、宾语或表语；every 和 no 只能作定语。例如：

— Do you have a pencil? 你有铅笔吗？

— Yes, I have one. 是的，我有一支。

I don't know any of them. 我不认识他们中的任何一个人。

7. 疑问代词

疑问代词有 who，whom，whose，what 和 which 等，在句子中用来构成特殊疑问句。疑问代词都可用作连接代词，引导名词性从句（主语从句、宾语从句和表语从句）。例如：

Tell me who he is. 告诉我他是谁。

8. 关系代词

关系代词有 who，whom，whose，that，which，as 等，可用作引导从句的关联词。它们在定语从句中可作主语、表语、宾语、定语等；同时，它们又代表主句中被定语从句所修饰的那个名词或代词（先行词）。例如：

He is the manager whom you will be working for. 他就是你将来的经理。

二、人称代词

1. 人称代词的用法

（1）人称代词的主格在句子中作主语或主语补语。例如：

The soldier waited a while but eventually he went home.

那个士兵等了一会儿，最后他回家了。

He hoped the passenger would be his sweetheart and indeed it was she.

他希望那位乘客是他的心上人，还真是她。

说明：在复合句中，如果主句和从句主语相同，代词主语要用在从句中，名词主语用在主句中。例如：

When he arrived, Tom went straight to the restaurant. 汤姆一到就直接进了饭店。

（2）人称代词的宾格在句子中作宾语或介词宾语，但在口语中也能作主语补语，第一人称在省略句中，还可以作主语。例如：

I saw her with them, at least, I thought it was her. 我看到她和他们在一起，至少我认为是她。（her 作宾语，them 作介词宾语，her 作主语补语）

— Who broke the cup? 谁打碎了杯子？

— Me. 我。（me 作主语补语 = It's me.）

说明：在上面的两个例句中，her 和 me 分别作主语和补语。现代英语中此处多用宾格，在正式文体中这里应为 she 和 I。

2. 人称代词的主宾格替换

（1）宾格代替主格。主要有下列两种情况。

① 在简短对话中，当人称代词单独使用或在 not 后，多用宾格。例如：

— I like English. 我喜欢英语。

— Me too. 我也喜欢。

— Have more Tea? 再来点茶喝吗？

— Not me. 我可不要了。

② 在表示比较的非正式文体中，常用宾格代替主格。但如果比较状语的谓语保留，则主语只能用主格。例如：

He is taller than I/me.

He is taller than I am.

（2）主格代替宾格。主要有下列两种情况。

① 在介词 but, except 后，有时可用主格代替宾格。

② 在电话用语中常用主格。例如：

— I wish to speak to Mr. Wang. 我想和王先生通话。

— This is he. 我就是。

3. 并列人称代词的排列顺序

（1）单数人称代词并列作主语时，其顺序为：第二人称→第三人称→第一人称，即 you→he/she/it→I。例如：

You, he and I should return on time.

（2）复数人称代词作主语时，其顺序为：第一人称→第二人称→第三人称，即 we→you→they。

注意：在下列情况中，第一人称放在前面。

①在承认错误、承担责任时，例如：

It was I and George that made the teacher angry. 是我和乔治惹老师生气了。

②在长辈对晚辈、长官对下属说话，长官为第一人称时，例如：

I and you try to work on it. 我和你去弄好它。

③并列主语只有第一人称和第三人称时。

④当其他人称代词或名词被定语从句修饰时。

三、代词的指代

（1）不定代词 anybody, everybody, nobody, anyone, someone, everyone, no one 以及 whoever 和 person 在正式场合使用时，可用 he, his, him 代替。例如：

Nobody came, did he? 谁也没来，是吗？

（2）动物名词的指代一般用 it 或 they，带有亲切的感情色彩时也用 he, she。例如：

Give the cat some food. She is hungry. 给这猫一些吃的。她饿了。

（3）指代车、船舶或国家的名词，含感情色彩时常用 she。

四、物主代词

1. 物主代词的作用

物主代词既有表示所属的作用，又有指代的作用。例如：

The computer is mine and mine is the latest model. 这部电脑是我的，是最新款。

物主代词有形容词性物主代词（my, your 等）和名词性物主代词（mine, yours 等）两种。形容词性物主代词属于限定词，名词性物主代词在用法上相当于省略了中心名词的 's 属格结构。例如：

his pen 意为 The pen is his。The shoes are Jack's. 可以说成 The shoes are his。

2. 名词性物主代词的句法功能

（1）作主语。例如：

May I use your pen? Yours works better. 我可以用一下你的钢笔吗？你的比我的好用。

（2）作宾语。例如：

I love my child as much as you love yours. 我爱我的孩子就像你爱你的孩子一样。

（3）作介词宾语。例如：

He is interested in my story, not in yours. 他想听我的故事，而不是你的故事。

（4）作主语补语。例如：

The life I have is yours. It's yours. It's yours. 我的生命属于你，属于你，属于你。

五、双重所有格

物主代词不可与 a, an, this, that, these, those, some, any, several, no, each, every, such, another, which 等词一起前置，修饰一个名词，而必须用双重所有格。公式为：a, an, this, that +名词+of +名词性物主代词。例如：

a friend of his 他的朋友　　each brother of hers 她的每个兄弟

六、反身代词

反身代词的数和人称的变化及其与人称代词的对应关系如表 2-3 所示。

表 2-3 反身代词人称和数的变化

数	单数			复数		
人称	第一人称	第二人称	第三人称	第一人称	第二人称	第三人称
人称代词	I	you	he/she/it	we	you	they
反身代词	myself	yourself	himself/herself/itself	ourselves	yourselves	themselves

另外，one 的反身代词为 oneself。

反身代词的句法功能如下：

（1）用作宾语。主要有以下两种用法：

① 有些动词后面可以接反身代词，如 absent, bathe, amuse, blame, dry, cut, enjoy, hurt, introduce, behave 等。例如：

We enjoyed ourselves very much last week. 我们上周玩得很开心。

Please help yourself to some fruit. 请你随便吃点水果。

② 用于"及物动词+宾语+介词"，如 take pride in, be annoyed with, help oneself to something 等。例如：

My mother dress (myself) up at that time. 那个时候我妈妈给我穿衣打扮。

注：有些动词后不跟反身代词，如：get up, sit down, stand up, wake up 等。例如：

Please sit down. 请坐。

（2）用作表语。例如：

Be yourself! 做你自己！

（3）用作同位语。例如：

The thing itself is not important. 事情本身并不重要。

（4）在不强调的情况下，but, except, for 等介词后的宾语用反身代词或人称代词宾格均可。例如：

No one but myself (me) is hurt. 除了我没人受伤。

注意：

① 反身代词本身不能单独作主语。

（错）Myself ride the bike.

（对）I myself ride the bike. 我自己骑自行车。

② 但在 and, or, nor 连接的并列主语中，第二个主语可用反身代词，特别是 myself。例如：

William and myself went to school. 威廉和我去了学校。

七、相互代词

相互代词只有 each other 和 one another 两个词组。它们表示句中动词所叙述的动作或感觉在涉及的各个对象之间是相互存在的。例如：

They come from different countries and respect each other.

他们来自不同的国家，相互尊重对方。

相互代词的句法功能如下：

（1）可作动词宾语。例如：

People should love one another. 人们应当彼此相爱。

（2）可作介词宾语。例如：

They talk to each other. 他们在聊天。

八、指示代词

指示代词分单数（this / that）和复数（these / those）两种形式，既可作限定词又可作代词（见表 2-4）。

表 2-4　指示代词的形式和作用

	单数	复数
限定词	This girl is Cindy.	Those men are my colleagues.
代词	This is Cindy.	Those are my colleagues.

指示代词的句法功能如下：

（1）作主语。例如：

This is the way to the cinema. 这就是去电影院的路。

（2）作宾语。例如：

I like that girl better than that boy. 我喜欢那个女孩胜过那个男孩。

（3）作主语补语。例如：

My idea is this. 我的观点就是如此。

（4）作介词宾语。例如：

I don't agree to that. 我不同意那个意见。

There is no fear of that. 那并不可怕。

说明：that 和 those 可作定语从句的先行词，但 this 和 these 不能。

（对）He likes that which looked attractive. 他喜欢外表漂亮的东西。

（对）He likes those who looked attractive. 他喜欢那些外表漂亮的人。

九、疑问代词

1. 疑问代词的作用

疑问代词在句中起名词词组的作用，用来构成疑问句。疑问代词有下列几个：

（1）指人：who, whom, whose；

（2）指物：what；

（3）既可指人又可指物：which。

2. 疑问代词的具体用法

疑问代词在句中应位于谓语动词之前，没有性和数的变化，除 who 之外也没有格的变化。what, which, whose 还可作限定词。例如：

疑问代词：Whose are these pens on the desk? 桌上的钢笔是谁的？

What was the task? 任务是什么？

限定词：Whose pens are these on the desk? 桌上的钢笔是谁的？

What events led to his failure in business? 哪些事件导致了他生意上的失败？

（1）无论是作疑问代词还是限定词，which 和 what 所指的范围不同。what 所指的范围是无限的，而 which 则指在一定的范围内。例如：

Which books do you like best? 你喜欢哪几本书？

What books do you like best? 你喜欢什么样的书？

(2) whom 是 who 的宾格，在书面语中，它作动词或介词的宾语，在口语中作宾语时，可用 who 代替，但在介词后只能用 whom。例如：

Who(m) did you tell? 你告诉谁了？（作动词宾语）

Who(m) did you buy the present for? 你给谁买礼物了？（作介词宾语，置于句首）

To whom did you speak in the office? 你在办公室里和谁讲话了？（作介词宾语，置于介词后，不能用 who 取代。）

(3) 疑问代词还可引导名词性从句。例如：

I can't figure out what his point is. 我不知道他用意何在。

Can you tell me whose is the red skirt? 你能告诉我那件红裙子是谁的吗？

十、关系代词

1. 关系代词的作用

关系代词用来引导定语从句。它代表先行词，同时在从句中作一定的句子成分。例如：

The girl to whom I spoke is my best friend. 跟我讲话的姑娘是我最好的朋友。

该句中 whom 既代表先行词 the girl，又在从句中作介词 to 的宾语。

2. 关系代词的用法

关系代词有主格、宾格和属格之分，并有指人与指物之分。在限定性定语从句中，that 既可指人也可指物。关系代词的用法总结见表 2-5。

表 2-5　关系代词的用法

	指人	指物	指人或指物
主 格	who	which	that
宾 格	whom	that	that
属 格	whose	of which/whose	of which/whose

例如：

This is the boy whose father is an alcoholic. 这就是父亲酗酒的那个孩子。（whose 指人，在限定性定语从句中作定语）

He came back for the keys which he had forgotten. 他回来取他的钥匙。（which 指物，在限定性定语从句中作宾语，可以省略）

说明：在非限定性定语从句中，不能用 that 作关系代词。

3. 关系代词 which

(1) 关系代词 which 的先行词可以是一个句子。例如：

He said he was an honest guy, which was a lie. 他说他是个诚实的人，这纯属谎言。

(2) 关系代词在从句中作宾语时可以省略。另外，关系代词 that 在从句中作表语时也可省略，例如：

He introduced me to several people I once heard of. 他把我介绍给几个我以前听说过的人物。

The town has changed. It is not the place it was. 这个地方变化很大，已不是过去的样子了。

Unit 2

练 习

I. 选择题。

1. My uncle gave a new camera to _____ as a birthday present.
   A. theirs   B. they   C. me   D. I
2. This is a photo of _____ family. May I have one of _____?
   A. yours; my   B. my; yours   C. your; my   D. yours; mine
3. —Here's a postcard for you, Jim! —Oh, _____ is from Mary.
   A. he   B. it   C. she   D. it's
4. They asked _____ some questions _____ English.
   A. me; about   B. I; about   C. I; with   D. me; with
5. Help _____ answer the questions.
   A. I   B. my   C. me   D. mine
6. These are my books. Where are _____?
   A. their   B. theirs   C. my   D. your
7. He has five children, and _____ of them is good at painting.
   A. everyone   B. everybody   C. every one   D. every
8. I have three brothers, _____ are in Beijing.
   A. no one of them   B. neither of them   C. some of them   D. none of them
9. Some of my students study a lot, _____ just don't care.
   A. anothers   B. the other   C. some other   D. others
10. As a matter of fact, Saudi Arabia's oil reserves are second only to _____.
    A. Kuweit   B. that of Kuweit
    C. Kuweits's   D. those of Kuweit
11. This book of _____ used to be one of the best sellers in the shop.
    A. his   B. him   C. that man   D. this
12. We should always keep _____ well-informed of the changing information.
    A. us   B. ours   C. ourselves   D. we
13. The climate here is often said to be similar to _____.
    A. Japan   B. one of Japan C. that of Japan   D. in Japan
14. Hunted by constant fear of arrest, the thief _____ to the police at last.
    A. gave it up   B. gave up himself
    C. gave him up   D. gave himself up
15. _____ of the boys in the class who have passed the test is to receive certificates.
    A. Every   B. Every one   C. Any   D. Anyone
16. Do you believe that she has blamed us for the accident, especially _____?
    A. you and me   B. you and I   C. I and you   D. me and you

17. Of those who graduated with _____, Ellen is the only one who has found a good job.

    A. Betty and he   B. he and Betty   C. Betty and him   D. him and Betty

18. He is surprised by _____ having to pay for the accident.

    A. you   B. yours   C. your   D. your's

19. This is a left hand glove and that is _____.

    A. other   B. the other one   C. other one   D. another

20. Add those examples to _____ you have already noted.

    A. ones   B. the one   C. one   D. the ones

II. 将括号内的人称代词变成适当的形式填空。

1. Our house is better than _____ (they).

2. I will give the presents to _____ (they).

3. These books are _____ (I), and those are _____ (you).

4. My ruler is long. _____ (you) is short.

5. My bike is broken. May I borrow _____ (she)?

6. Can you show _____ (I) your book?

7. It's time for _____ (they) to go home.

8. Mr. Green often tells _____ (we) some stories.

9. These are not your desks. They are _____ (our).

10. This is not my shirt. It's _____ (he).

Part Seven   Writing

Greeting Cards

Directions: In this part, you are going to learn how to write a *Greeting Card* and then try your hand.

1. Read the following samples.

Sample 1

> To Mr. and Mrs. Owen
>
>   Merry Christmas and Happy New Year
>   With best wishes and regards
>   May you happy everyday
>
>   from Annie

Sample 2

> To Dear Li Fang
>
> Congratulations on Your Success
> In the College Entrance Examination
>
> from Wang Li

2. A) **Write a greeting card to your mother on Mother's Day.**

B) **Write a greeting card to your friend Liu Qiang to congratulate on his...**

Data Bank

Merry Christmas!	圣诞节快乐!
Happy Birthday to you!	生日快乐!
Happy New Year!	新年好!
Happy Valentine's Day!	情人节快乐!
Happy Mother's Day!	母亲节快乐!
Happy Father's Day!	父亲节快乐!
Congratulations on your Wedding Anniversary!	恭贺结婚周年!
Congratulations on your happy day!	恭贺新婚之喜!
Best wishes to you both!	新婚美满幸福!
Congratulations on the birth of your new baby!	恭喜喜得贵子!
Congratulations on your marriage and best wishes to you both.	恭贺新婚,祝福美满!
Good luck with you!	祝你好运!

Tips

制作用于表示美好祝愿的节日或喜庆日英语贺卡,要写清楚收卡人(recipient)的姓名、贺词(message)以及送卡人(sender)的名字。注意:收卡人姓名前面的介词 To 的第一个字母要大写,而送卡人名字前面的介词 from 的第一个字母要小写。

Culture Notes

1. Reading makes a full man; conference, a ready man; writing, an exact man.
   — Francis Bacon

2. If one cannot enjoy reading a book over and over again, there is no use in reading it at all.
   — Oscar Wilde

3. Today a reader, tomorrow a leader.
   — Margaret Fuller

4. A home without books is a body without soul.
   — Marcus Tullius Cicero

5. To learn to read is to light a fire; every syllable that is spelled out is a spark.
   — Victor Hugo

Unit 3

Generation

 Part One　Warm-up

1. What are the characteristics of young people? Please list some.

2. Do you think many young people are satisfied with their lives? If not, what do they usually do to express their true feelings?
3. What kind of life do you think young people would like to live?
4. Do you know some youth subcultures? Please give some examples.

Part Two Speaking and Listening

Section A Listen to the following conversation and then repeat.

Son: Mom, you know that Andrea and I sometimes worry about you.

Mom: Really? Why would you worry about me? I'm just fine.

Son: You're almost 70 years old, Mom! Don't you think it would be better for you if you moved in with us?

Mom: No way! I like my apartment, and I like to be independent.

Son: Do you ever get lonely living alone?

Mom: Not at all. I see you and your family twice a week, and I enjoy seeing my own friends. I'm too busy to feel lonely!

Section B Listen to the following short passage and fill in the missing words.

My problem is my mom and I fight over everything, such as dinner, clothes, boyfriends, money. I'll try to just walk away from the fight, but then she follows me and gets even more 1) _____. I try to stay 2) _____, but when you have a woman yelling at you for no 3) _____ reason, it can get pretty tricky. Our fighting put a lot of unneeded 4) _____ on me. I understand that she is under a lot of stress from her job and money, etc., but that's no reason for her to take it out on me. Ugh. It'll 5) _____ pass, but I'd like to go through this phase as fast as I can.

Part Three Detailed Reading

Generation Y: They've Arrived at Work with a New Attitude

They're young and smart. They may wear flip-flops to the office or listen to iPods at their desk. They want to work, but they don't want work to be their life.

This is Generation Y, a force of as many as 70 million, and the first wave is just now starting their careers. Get ready, because this generation — whose members have not yet reached 30 years old — is different from any that have come before.

Work-life balance isn't just a buzzword. Unlike older generations who tend to put a high priority on career, today's youngest workers are more interested in making their jobs fit their family and personal lives. They want jobs with flexibility. They want the ability to go part time or leave the workforce temporarily when children are in the picture.

"There's a higher value on self-fulfillment," says Diana San Diego, 24, who lives with her parents in San Francisco and works on college campuses. "After 9/11, there is a realization that life is short. You value it more."

Change, change, change. Generation Yers don't expect to stay in a job, or even a career, for too long — they've seen the scandals that ruined Enron and Arthur Andersen, and they're doubtful when it comes to such ideas as employee loyalty.

They don't like to stay too long on any one assignment. This is a generation of multitaskers, and they can manage to send e-mail on their BlackBerrys while talking on cellphones while surfing online.

And they believe in their own self-worth and value. They're not shy about trying to change the companies they work for. That compares somewhat with Gen X, a generation born from the mid-1960s to the late-1970s, known for its independent thinking, addiction to change and emphasis on family.

Conflicts over casual dress and management style. In the workplace, conflict and resentment can arise over a lot of issues, even seemingly minor subjects such as appearance, as a generation used to casual things such as flip-flops, tattoos and capri pants.

Angie Ping, 23, of Alvin, Texas, lives in flip-flops but isn't allowed to wear them to the office. He says, "The new trend for work dress this season is menswear-inspired capri pants, which look as dressy as pants when paired with heels, but capri pants are not allowed at my organization."

Conflict can also emerge over management style. Unlike previous generations who've in large part grown accustomed to the annual review, Gen Yers have grown up getting constant feedback and recognition from teachers, parents and coaches. If there isn't regular communication with bosses, they will feel lost. So it is time for them to solve those conflicts.

Generation Y is different from other generations. They hold a new attitude toward work: they have conflicting ideas about matters but try to strike a balance between things.

(This text is adapted from the website http://www.usatoday.com, 2012-01-13.)

New Words

generation	[ˌdʒenəˈreiʃən]	n.	all the people living at the same time or of about the same age 代，一代
smart	[smɑːt]	adj.	characterized by quickness and ease in learning 聪明的
flip-flop	[ˈflipflɔp]	n.	夹趾拖鞋
buzzword	[ˈbʌzwəːd]	n.	a word or phrase related to a particular subject, that has become fashionable and popular and is used a lot in newspapers 时髦词语，漂亮口号
priority	[praiˈɔriti]	n.	status established in order of importance or urgency 优先权
flexibility	[ˌfleksəˈbiliti]	n.	ability to change to suit different needs or situations 灵活性
temporarily	[ˈtempərərili]	adv.	for a limited time only 暂时地，临时地
self-fulfillment	[ˌselfulˈfilmənt]	n.	the fulfillment of your capacities 自我实现
scandal	[ˈskændl]	n.	a disgraceful event 丑闻，丑行
ruin	[ruin]	v.	to destroy or cause to fail 毁灭，毁坏
loyalty	[ˈlɔiəlti]	n.	the quality of being faithful in your support of somebody or something 忠诚，忠实
assignment	[əˈsainmənt]	n.	a duty that you are assigned to perform （分派的）工作，任务
multitask	[ˌmʌltiˈtæsk]	vt.	to work at several different tasks simultaneously (multitasker n.) 使多任务化
addiction	[əˈdikʃən]	n.	the state of being addicted or a habit to which one is addicted 上瘾，入迷
conflict	[ˈkɔnflikt]	n.	a state of opposition between persons, ideas or interests 矛盾，抵触，不一致
casual	[ˈkæʒjuəl]	adj.	not formal 非正式的，随便的
resentment	[riˈzentmənt]	n.	a feeling of deep and bitter anger and ill-will 怨恨，愤恨
tattoo	[tæˈtuː]	n.	a pattern or a picture put on the skin by tattooing 文身
capri pants			卡普里裤，七分裤
inspire	[inˈspaiə]	v.	to give somebody the idea for something especially something artistic or that shows imagination 赋予灵感，引起联想
dressy	[ˈdresi]	adj.	in fancy clothing 衣着华丽的
emerge	[iˈməːdʒ]	v.	to come out of a dark, confined or hidden place 出现，浮现

accustomed	[əˈkʌstəmd]	*adj.*	familiar with something and accepting it as normal or usual 习惯于
feedback	[ˈfiːdbæk]	*n.*	advice, criticism or information about how good or useful something or somebody's work is 反馈

Phrases & Expressions

1. **in the picture**: including somebody; involving somebody in a situation 包括某人，让某人参与
   例：I haven't heard about the latest developments; perhaps you could put me in the picture. 我没有听到最新的发展情况，也许你能告诉我详情。

2. **when it comes to**: when it is a question of 当谈到……，涉及……
   例：When it comes to getting things done, he's useless. 一涉及做事，他就不中用了。

3. **compare with/to**: similar to somebody/something else, either better or worse 与……相比
   例：I've had some difficulties, but they were nothing compared with/to yours. 我遇到了一些困难，但与你的困难比起来就不算什么了。

4. **be/get used to something**: in the habit of; be/get accustomed to 习惯于……
   例：I found the job tiring at first but I soon got used to it. 起初我觉得这份工作很累人，但很快就习惯了。

Comprehension of the Text

Answer the following questions according to the text.

1. What are the characteristics making Generation Y different from any that have come before?
2. How does this young generation deal with the relationship between work and life?
3. What's Generation Y's attitude towards such ideas as employee loyalty?
4. Why Generation Y is called a generation of multitaskers?
5. What are the conflicts Generation Y has to face in their working life?

 Part Four Exercises

Task 1 Choose the definition from Column B that best matches each word or phrase in Column A.

A	B
1. scandal	a. the quality of being faithful in your support of somebody or something
2. feedback	b. not formal
3. inspire	c. advice, criticism about how good or useful something or something's work is
4. conflict	d. status established in order of importance or urgency
5. priority	e. to give somebody the idea for something, especially something artistic or that shows imagination
6. compare with	f. a word or phrase related to a particular subject, that has become fashionable and popular and is used a lot in newspapers
7. loyalty	g. a disgraceful event
8. accustomed	h. similar to somebody or something else, either better or worse
9. buzzword	i. a state of opposition between persons, ideas or interests
10. casual	j. familiar with something and accepting it as normal or usual

Task 2 Fill in the blanks with the words or expressions given below. Change the form where necessary.

accustomed	conflict	emerge	priority	when it comes to
feedback	inspire	temporarily	casual	addiction

1. We need both positive and negative _____ from our customers.
2. You will soon get _____ to the climate here.
3. He is now trying his best to fight his _____ to drugs.
4. His best music was _____ by the memory of his mother.
5. The serious _____ between the employers and workers led to the strike last week.
6. _____ education, most people believe that education is a lifetime study.
7. Finally the truth of the matter _____.
8. Such _____ dress would not be correct for a formal occasion.
9. The daily flight to the city has been _____ stopped because of the earthquake.
10. The Government gave top _____ to reforming the legal system.

42

Unit 3

Task 3 Translate the following sentences into English, paying special attention to the underlined parts.

1. 这房子不如我们以前的。(compare with)
2. 我不习惯吃辛辣食品。(be used to)
3. 太阳从云层后面露出来了。(emerge)
4. 谈到日语，我一窍不通。(when it comes to)
5. 她是职业女性而不是家庭主妇。(career woman)

Part Five Supplementary Reading

Emo Youth Were Attacked

On March 7th, 2008, an estimated 800 young people poured into the City of Mexico hunting for emos to beat them. They found some. The ugly scene, which was broadcast on TV news, is part of a new wave of violence against this urban tribe that has developed in Mexico in the last decade. The emo subculture probably existed in your high school before the term even bloomed, and the latest movement was represented by goths in the 1980s and rockers in the 1990s. In yearbooks, they're the kids who wear exaggerated haircuts and immerse themselves in sad music. In short: the kids have been beating up for decades.

Emos are one of the colorful youth cultures popular in the U.S. and Europe. They have swept over the Rio Grande as the nation opens up and a new generation grows up with the Internet and cable TV. Punks, goths, rockabillies, breakdancers, skaters and metallers all now pace Mexican streets, decorate the squares and spray paint on the walls. But while most of the trends have met with an unwilling acceptance, emos have provoked a violent backlash. It is reported that a mob also attacked emos in the heart of Mexico City earlier this month. Furthermore, emos complain they are being increasingly threatened and attacked by smaller groups on the streets on a daily basis. "It's getting dangerous for us to go out now. We get shouted at and spat on. We get things thrown at us. There is so much hate out there," said a 16-year-old emo high school student sitting in a Mexico City square alongside other teenagers in tight black jeans and dark makeup.

The attackers, regarded as "anti-emos," include some from other urban tribes such as punks and metallers, but many are just ordinary working-class teenagers and young men. They mock the emos for being posers who are overly sentimental and accuse them of robbing from other music forms. With roots in Washington, D. C., in the 1980s, emo bands play a style of rock that borrows much from punk and rock. They focus on exploring their emotions (hence the name) with a particular dwelling on typical teenage depression.

(This text is adapted from *http：//www.time.com*, 2011-11-10.)

New Words

estimate	[ˈestimeit]	n.	an approximate calculation of quantity, degree or worth 估计
violence	[ˈvaiələns]	n.	an act of aggression (as one against a person who resists) 暴力
tribe	[traib]	n.	a group or class of people, especially of one profession 一伙人，一帮人
decade	[ˈdekeid]	n.	a period of ten years 十年
bloom	[bluːm]	v.	to be in a healthy growing state; flourish 兴旺，繁盛
yearbook	[ˈjiəˌbuk]	n.	a book published once a year, giving details of events of the previous year 年鉴，年刊
exaggerated	[igˈzædʒəreitid]	adj.	enlarged to an abnormal degree 夸张的，夸大的
immerse	[iˈməːs]	v.	to become or make somebody completely involved in something 沉浸在……
spray	[sprei]	v.	to cover something with very small drops of a liquid that are forced out of a container or sent through the air 喷，喷洒
provoke	[prəˈvəuk]	v.	to cause a particular reaction or have a particular effect 激起，引起，引发
backlash	[ˈbæklæʃ]	n.	a strong negative reaction by a large number of people 强烈抵制，集体反对
spit	[spit]	v.	to force something out of your mouth 吐，吐痰
makeup	[ˈmeikʌp]	n.	colored substances that are put on your face to improve or

			change your appearance 化妆品
mock	[mɔk]	v.	to laugh at 嘲笑，嘲弄
poser	[ˈpəuzə]	n.	someone who pretends to have a quality or social position 装腔作势的人
sentimental	[ˌsentiˈmentl]	adj.	easily affected by emotions such as love, sympathy 感伤性的，感情脆弱的
depression	[diˈpreʃən]	n.	a medical condition that makes you very unhappy and anxious 沮丧，抑郁

Phrases & Expressions

1. **on a daily basis**：everyday，each day 每天

   例：These workers are paid on a daily basis. 这些工人领的是日薪。

2. **dwell on**：to think for a long time about something 老是想……

   例：They didn't dwell on their failures. 他们不会对自己的失败念念不忘。

Comprehension of the Text

Answer the following questions according to the text.

1. What's emo youth culture?
2. Why are many people dissatisfied with emo youth and want to attack them?
3. What do you know about some other subcultures besides emo youth subculture?

 Part Six　Grammar

代词（Pronouns）（二）

上一课中我们讲了八种代词中的七种，本课中介绍剩下的一种——不定代词。

不指明代替任何特定名词的代词叫做不定代词。常见的不定代词有 all, both, every, each, either, neither, more, little, few, much, many, another, other, some, any, one, no 以及 something, anything, everything, somebody, someone, anybody, anyone, nothing, nobody, no one, none, everybody, everyone 等。

这些不定代词大都可以代替名词和形容词，在句中作主语、宾语、表语和定语，但 none 和由 some, any, no 等构成的复合不定代词只能作主语、宾语或表语；every 和 no 只能

作定语。

一、every, no, all, both, neither, nor 的相关用法

1. all, every, no 的相关用法

all 表示全部都，no 表示全部否定，every 与 not 连用时表示部分否定。

（1）除 every 和 no 外，不定代词既可用作名词，也可用作形容词。every 和 no 在句中只能作定语。例如：

I have no idea about it. 我不知该怎么办。

（2）all 表示都，指三者以上。all 的单复数由它所修饰或指代的名词的单复数决定。例如：

All is well that ends well. 最终好了，一切也就好了。

all 通常不与可数名词单数连用，比如，不说 all the nation，而说 the whole nation。

但 all 可与表时间的可数名词单数连用，如：all day, all night, all the year；但习惯上不说 all hour, all century。

all 还可以与一些特殊的单数名词连用，如：all China, all the city, all my life。

2. both（都，指两者）的相关用法

（1）both 与复数名词连用，但 both...and...可与单数名词连用。

（2）both, all 都可作同位语，其位置在行为动词前，be 动词之后。如果助动词或情态动词后面的实义动词省去，则位于助动词或情态动词之前。例如：

— Who can dance? 谁能跳舞？

— We both（all）can. 我们都会。

3. neither（两者都不）的相关用法

（1）neither 作主语时，谓语动词用单数。

（2）作定语与单数名词连用，但 neither...nor 用作并列连词，可与复数名词连用。其谓语采用就近原则。

（3）可用于下列句型，以避免重复。例如：

She can't play the piano, neither（can）he. 她不会弹琴，他也不会。

4. neither 与 nor 的比较

（1）如果前句是否定句，则后句用 neither，而不用 nor。例如：

He doesn't like fish; neither do I. 他不喜欢吃鱼，我也不喜欢。

（2）如果后面连续有几个否定句式，则用 nor，不用 neither。例如：

He can't read, nor write, nor sing. 他不会读，不会写，也不会唱。

二、none, few, any, some, one, ones 的相关用法

1. none（无）的相关用法

（1）none 作主语，多与 of 构成短语 none of。在答语中，none 可单独使用。例如：

— Are there any CDs in the library? 图书馆里有 CD 吗？

— None. 没有。

（2）none 作主语，谓语动词单复数均可。但如作表语，则其单复数与表语一致。例如：

It is none of your business. 闲事莫管。

2. few（一些，少数）的相关用法

few 作主语时，谓语动词用复数，多用于肯定句。

3. any（一些）的相关用法

（1）any 多用于否定句、疑问句和条件状语从句中。

（2）当句中含有"任何"的意思时，any 可用于肯定句。例如：

Here are three story books. You may read any. 这里有三本故事书，你可任读一本。

4. some（一些）的相关用法

（1）可与复数名词及不可数名词连用。

（2）当作"某一"解时，也可与单数名词连用。（= a certain）

You will regret some day. 总有一天，你会为此后悔的。

A certain (Some) person has seen you steal the wallet. 有人看到你偷钱包了。

（3）some 用于下列句式中。

①用于肯定疑问句中，即说话人认为对方的答案会是肯定的，或期望得到肯定的回答时，用 some 代替 any。

②在 Would you like…句式中，表委婉的请求或建议。例如：

Would you like some tea? 喝茶吗？

③在条件状语从句中，表示确定的意义时。例如：

If you need some help, you can turn to your teacher. 如需帮助，找你的老师。

④some 位于否定句的主语部分。例如：

Some students haven't handed in their assignment. 有些学生没有交作业。

⑤当否定的是整体中的部分时，some 可用于否定句。例如：

I haven't heard from some of my old colleagues these years. 这些年我没有收到一些老同事的信。

5. one（复数形式为 ones）的相关用法

ones 必须和形容词连用。如果替代的名词前无形容词，则用 some，any，而不用 ones。例如：

— Have you bought any apples? 买苹果了吗？

— Yes, I've bought some. 买了，买了一些。

三、one，that 和 it 的相关用法

one 表示泛指，that 和 it 表示特指。that 与所指名词为同类，但不是同一个，而 it 与所指名词为同一个。例如：

I can't find my pen. I think I must buy one.（不定）我找不到我的钢笔了。我想我该去买一支。

The pen you bought writes better than that I bought.（同类但不同一个）你买的那支钢笔比我的好用。

I can't find my pen. I don't know where I put it.（同一物）我找不到我的钢笔。我不知道我把它放在哪了。

四、one，another 和 the other 的相关用法

常用搭配是：one…the other（只有两个）；some…the others（有三个以上）；one…another，another…；some…others，others…其中 others = other people/things，the others = the rest（剩余的全部）。

（1）泛指另一个，用 another。

（2）一定范围内的两个人或物，一个用 one 指代，另一个用 the other 指代。

（3）一定范围内的三者，一个用 one 指代，另一个用 one（another）指代，第三个可用 the other，a third 指代。

（4）一定范围内，除去一部分人或物，剩余的全部用 the others 指代。

（5）泛指别的人或物时，用 others 指代；在一定范围内，除去一部分人或物，剩余部分但不是全部，也用 others 指代。

五、the 的妙用

He is one of the teachers who help me. 他是帮我的老师之一。

He is the one of the teachers who helps me. 他是帮过我的那个老师。

第一句定语从句与 the teachers 一致。

第二句定语从句与 the one 一致。

六、anyone/any one，no one/none 和 every/each 的相关用法

1. anyone 和 any one 的相关用法

anyone 仅指人，any one 既可指人，也可指物。

2. no one 和 none 的相关用法

（1）none 后跟 of 短语，既可指人又可指物，而 no one 只能单独使用，只指人。

（2）none 作主语，谓语动词用单、复数均可，而 no one 作主语时谓语动词只能是单数。

例如：

None of you could tackle the problem. 你们中没有人能解决这个问题。

— Did any one look for me just now? 刚才有人找我吗？

— No one. 没有。

3. every 和 each 的相关用法

（1）every 强调全体的概念，each 强调个体的概念。例如：

Every citizen in this country respect the president. 这个国家所有的市民都很尊重那位总统。

Each student may have one free gift. 每个学生都可免费领取一份礼物。

（2）every 指三个以上的人或物（含三个），each 指两个以上的人或物（含两个）。

（3）every 只作形容词，不可单独使用；each 可作代词或形容词。例如：

Every girl has to take one. 每个女孩必须取一个。

Each girl has to take one.

Each of the girls has to take one.

（4）every 不可以作状语，each 可作状语。

（5）every 有反复重复的意思，如 every two weeks 等；each 没有。

（6）every 与 not 连用，表示部分否定；each 和 not 连用，表示全部否定。例如：

Every citizen is not honest. 并非每个人都诚实。

Each citizen is not honest. 每个人都不诚实。

七、both, either, neither, all, any, none 的相关用法

这些词都可用作代词或形容词，其位置都在 be 动词之后，行为动词之前，或第一个助

动词之后。

1. both，either，neither 的相关用法

（1）both（两者都）、either（两者中任何一个）、neither（两者都不）的使用范围为两个人或物。例如：

Neither of the two students work hard. 两个学生学习都不用功。

（2）both 与复数连用，either 与单数连用。例如：

Both the students work hard. 两个学生学习很用功。

Either of the two students work hard. 两个学生学习很用功。

There are flowers on both sides of the bank. 河边长满了野花。

There are flowers on either side of the bank. 河边长满了野花。

2. all，any，none 的相关用法

all（所有的，全部的人或物），any（任何一个），none（都不）的使用范围为三者以上。例如：

All the workers are gone. 所有的工人都走了。

I don't like any of the workers. 这些工人我都不喜欢。

I like none of the workers. 这些工人我都不喜欢。

注意：all 与 none 用法一样：跟单数名词，用单数动词；跟复数名词，用复数动词。例如：

All of the teachers are there. 所有的老师都在那儿。

All (of) the coffee is there. 所有的咖啡都在那儿。

八、many，much 的相关用法

many，much 都意为"许多"，many 后接可数名词，much 后接不可数名词。例如：

How many people are there in the cinema? 多少人去看电影了？

How much money has been left? 还剩多少钱？

Many of the managers were at the meeting. 许多经理在开会。

Much of the time was spent on drawing. 画画花了许多时间。

九、few，little，a few，a little 的相关用法

（a）few 后接可数名词，（a）little 后接不可数名词。a few / a little 为肯定含义，意为"还有一点"。few / little 为否定含义，意为"没有多少了"。例如：

He has a few stamps. 他有几张邮票。

He has few stamps. 他几乎没有邮票。

We still have a little money left. 我们还有点儿钱。

There is little money left. 几乎没剩下什么钱了。

固定搭配：only a few (=few)，not a few (=many)，quite a few (=many)，many a (=many)。例如：

Many dictionaries were sold. /Many a dictionary was sold. 卖出了许多字典。

练 习

I. 选择题。

1. Shakespeare is the greatest English writer — will there ever be such _____?
   A. other　　　B. the other　　　C. another　　　D. other one

2. He was holding the wheel with one hand and waving with _____.
   A. other　　　B. the other　　　C. another　　　D. others'

3. I can't do the fourth and fifth questions but I've done _____.
   A. all　　　B. all others　　　C. all the other　　　D. all the others

4. What would you do if _____ tried to rob you in the street?
   A. someone　　　B. no one　　　C. none　　　D. any

5. Can you ask _____ to help you? I'm really busy.
   A. someone else　B. everyone else　C. else someone　D. else everyone

6. Don't just stand there, do _____!
   A. something　　　B. everything　　　C. anything　　　D. nothing

7. _____ likes money, but money is not _____.
   A. Everyone, everything
   B. Anyone, anything
   C. Someone, nothing
   D. Nobody, everything

8. There have been a lot of accidents in the fog. I read about _____ this morning.
   A. it　　　B. one　　　C. that　　　D. another

9. Many local businesses are having difficulties, and _____ have even gone bankrupt.
   A. many　　　B. some　　　C. others　　　D. the others

10. Oxford is not far from Stratford, so you can easily visit _____ in a day.
    A. both　　　B. any　　　C. either　　　D. all

11. Always check the details carefully before you sign _____ written agreement.
    A. any　　　B. either　　　C. neither　　　D. some

12. The universities have shown _____, if any, signs of a willingness to change.
    A. few　　　B. any　　　C. little　　　D. much

13. I can't find my pen, has _____ seen it?
    A. anyone　　　B. no one　　　C. everyone　　　D. none

14. "Is there any bread left?" "No, _____ at all."
    A. no one　　　B. neither　　　C. not　　　D. none

15. We can offer a comfortable home to a young person of _____ sex.
    A. both　　　B. any　　　C. neither　　　D. either

16. They're all free, take _____ you like.
    A. it　　　B. either　　　C. any　　　D. that

17. _____ of the students had done their homework but most hadn't.

A. Some   B. All   C. None   D. Both

18. "Would you like some more tea?" "Just _____ ."

    A. little   B. a little   C. few   D. a few

19. The man sat in the back of the car with a policeman on _____ side.

    A. both   B. any   C. all   D. either

20. I can't find the pen I was given. Have you seen _____ ?

    A. one   B. it   C. that   D. another

Ⅱ．把下列短语或句子翻译成中文。

1. a day or two

2. more than a year

3. a ten years

4. once upon a time

5. A cow is a domestic animal.

6. be of an age

7. once a year

8. need a wash

9. We need a washing today.

10. I have got a complete Shakespeare at hand.

Part Seven   Writing

Public Signs

Directions：In this part, you are going to learn how to make a *Public Sign* and then try your hand.

1. Read the following samples.

> Parking
> 2 Hours Free
> Entrance

> 停车处
> 两小时内免费
> 入口

2. Exercise：Translate the following English signs into Chinese with the help of a dictionary.

> Wet Floor
> Entrance
> Booking Office
> Two-way Street
> Keep off the Lawn
> No Spitting
> No Parking
> Staff Only
> Handle with Care
> Silence
> Hands off
> Road Construction Ahead

Data Bank

One Way Only	单行线
No Entrance	闲人免进
Not Open to Visitors	谢绝参观
Out of Bounds	禁止入内
No Admittance	禁止入内
Keep Your Hands off	请勿动手
No Photos	禁止拍照
No Smoking	禁止吸烟
Keep to the Right	靠右行走
Wet Paint	油漆未干
Keep off the Grass	勿进草地
No Littering	请勿乱扔废物

Tips

制作英语公共告示牌时，必须照顾到以英语为母语者的感受。因此，要注意模仿甚至"照搬"英语国家的惯用标识。切忌想当然"硬"译，如画蛇添足，将公厕（Toilet）译成"Public Toilet（公共公厕）"；或草率用词，将注意防火"Be Careful of Fire"译作"Take Care of Fire"（照顾好火）。

Unit 3

Culture Notes

Emo: (美国的一种非主流亚文化)	short for "emotional", an evolving and complex American youth subculture that listens to a specific form of music. Emo music draws from various forms of contemporary music including rock, rap, punk, indie, pop, and heavy metal. The behaviors, attitudes, and values expressed through the music involve emotionally turbulent themes often associated with adolescence such as despair, nostalgia（怀旧）, heartbreak, hope, and self-loathing（憎恨自己）.
punk: (朋克)	(1) a type of loud and aggressive rock music popular in the late 1970s and early 1980s. (2) a person who likes punk music and dresses like a punk musician, for example by wearing metal chains, leather clothes and having brightly colored hair.
goth: (哥特派)	(1) a style of rock music, popular in the 1980s, that developed from PUNK music. The word often expresses ideas about the end of the world, death or the devil. (2) a member of a group of people who listen to goth music and wear black clothes and black and white make-up. 哥特摇滚乐；哥特派中的一员
rocker: (摇滚青年)	a member of a group of young people in Britain, especially in the 1960s, who liked to wear leather jackets, ride motorcycles and listen to rock and roll.
rockabilly: (乡村摇滚乐)	a type of American music that combines rock and roll with country music.
breakdancer: (霹雳舞者)	a dancer of a style of dancing with acrobatic movements, often performed in the street.
metaller: (重金属音乐爱好者)	a group of young people in the 80s and early 90s, and they love to hold rock concerts, only ever wear band T-shirts, have very long hair and wear a chain on their jeans.

Unit 4

Friendship

Part One   Warm-up

1. Think of terms to describe friends or friendship and put them in the following box.

```


```

2. Who is your best friend? Say something about him/her.
3. Can you tell some stories about friendship?
4. Do you think friendship is very important in one's life? Why?

Unit 4

Part Two Speaking and Listening

Section A Listen to the following conversation and then repeat.

Sandy: When can we expect you for dinner? Can you come tonight?
Tom: Not tonight. I promised to go to a concert with my sister.
Sandy: Well... How about Friday then?
Tom: That sounds fine.
Sandy: Good. Shall we say seven o'clock?
Tom: I'll be there! You're still an excellent cook, aren't you?
Sandy: That'll be for you to decide. I've got a new dish that I want to try out on you.
Tom: I'm ready. I think I'll fast（禁食）all day Friday!

Section B Listen to the following short passage and fill in the missing words.

   Tales and stories about friends are told time and again to kids, in order to let them understand the true meaning of friendship. Such stories help them know how 1) _____ true friends are. Friendship is a relationship 2) _____ of mixed emotions. Friends would cry together, 3) _____ happiness and sorrow together, and have a lot of fun. Friends would bring a broad smile on our face and wipe all our tears. The moments spent with pals would often bring out a number of funny 4) _____, which would be 5) _____ for the lifetime.

Part Three Detailed Reading

True Friendship

Have you ever wondered what the real essence of the saying "A Friend in Need is a Friend Indeed" is? People talk about the true value of friendship actually without knowing what it stands for.

True friendship means that the individuals do not have to maintain formalities with each other. Sharing true friendship is the situation when the person you are talking about is counted as one among your family members. The relation you share with him/her reaches a stage that even if you don't write to or call him/her some time, your friendship remains unharmed. Best friends need not meet up often to make sure that the friendship remains constant.

The trust between best friends is such that if one friend falls in trouble, the other will not think twice to help. If the bond between two friends is strong, true friends can endure even long distances. For them, geographical separation is just a part of life. It would not affect their friendship. True friendship never fades away. In fact, it grows better with time. True friendship thrives on trust, inspiration and comfort. Best friends come to know, when the other person is in trouble, merely by listening to their "Hello" over the phone. They can even understand each other's silence.

True friends don't desert each other when one is facing trouble. They would face it together and support each other, even if it is against the interests of the other person. Best friends don't analyze each other; they don't have to do so. They accept each other with their positive and negative qualities. Nothing is hidden between true friends. They know each other's strengths as well as weaknesses. They would respect each other's individuality. In fact, they would understand the similarities and respect the differences. Best friends don't stand any outsider commenting or criticizing their friendship. If anyone does so, they can put up a very firm resistance.

True friends are not opportunists. They don't help, because they have something to gain out of it. True friendship is marked by selflessness. Best friends support each other, even if the whole world opposes them. It is not easy getting true friends for the lifetime. If you have even one true friend, consider yourself blessed. Remember, all best friends are friends, but not all friends can be best friends.

(This text is adapted from http://festivals.iloveindia.com, 2012-01-29.)

New Words

wonder	[ˈwʌndə]	v.	to have a wish or desire to know something 想知道
essence	[ˈesns]	n.	the most basic and important quality of something 精髓

Unit 4

individual	[ˌindiˈvidjuəl]	n.	a person, considered separately from the rest of the group or society that they live in 个人，个体
maintain	[meinˈtein]	v.	to keep in a certain state, position, or activity 维持
formality	[fɔːˈmæliti]	n.	something that you must do as a formal or official part of an activity or process 礼节，程序
count	[kaunt]	v.	to consider somebody/something in a particular way; to calculate 认为，视为；计算
constant	[ˈkɔnstənt]	adj.	happening regularly or all the time 经常的，不变的
bond	[bɔnd]	n.	something that unites two or more people or groups, such as love, or a shared interest or idea 联系，关系
endure	[inˈdjuə]	v.	to put up with something or somebody unpleasant 忍耐，容忍
geographical	[ˌdʒiːəˈgræfikl]	adj.	of or relating to the science of geography 地理的，地理学的
affect	[əˈfekt]	v.	to have an effect upon 影响
thrive	[θraiv]	v.	to grow stronger 兴旺，繁荣，茁壮成长
inspiration	[ˌinspəˈreiʃən]	n.	a person or thing that stimulates in this way 鼓舞人心的人或事物
comfort	[ˈkʌmfət]	n.	a state of being relaxed and feeling no pain 舒适，安慰
merely	[ˈmiəli]	adv.	and nothing more 仅仅，只不过
desert	[diˈzəːt]	v.	to leave someone or something and no longer help or support them 遗弃
analyze	[ˈænəlaiz]	v.	to examine or think about something carefully, in order to understand it 分析，解析
positive	[ˈpɔzətiv]	adj.	having the quality of something good and pleasant 肯定的，积极的，正面的
negative	[ˈnegətiv]	adj.	having the quality of something harmful or unpleasant 否定的，负的，消极的
quality	[ˈkwɔliti]	n.	something that people may have as part of their character, for example, courage or intelligence 品质，特质
individuality	[ˌindiˌvidʒuˈæləti]	n.	the qualities that make someone or something different from other things or people 个性，人格，特征
similarity	[ˌsimiˈlæriti]	n.	the quality of being similar 相似，类似
comment	[ˈkɔment]	v.	to express an opinion about someone or something 评论
criticize	[ˈkritisaiz]	v.	to express your disapproval of someone or something, or to talk about their faults 批评
resistance	[riˈzistəns]	n.	the action of opposing something 抵抗力，反抗
opportunist	[ˈɔpətjuːnist]	n.	someone who uses every opportunity to gain power, money, or unfair advantages 机会主义者，投机者

oppose	[əˈpəuz]	v.	to disagree with something such as a plan or idea and try to prevent it from happening or succeeding 反对，反抗
bless	[bles]	v.	to ask God to protect someone or something 保佑，祝福

Phrases & Expressions

1. **stand for**: to express indirectly by an image, form, or model; be a symbol 代表，象征
   例：What does "ESL" stand for? "ESL" 代表什么？
2. **meet up**: to meet somebody, especially by arrangement 约见，会见
   例：I met up with him/We met up at the supermarket. 我和他见了面。/我们在超市相遇。
3. **fade away**: to become weaker 逐渐消失；褪色
   例：The airliner faded away into the mist. 客机逐渐消失在雾中。
4. **put up resistance**: to fight against someone who is attacking 进行抵抗
   例：Rebel gunmen have put up strong resistance. 叛军枪手进行顽强的抵抗。

Comprehension of the Text

Choose the best answer for each of the following questions.

1. Which of the following is TRUE according to the first paragraph? _____
   A. True friends have to maintain formalities with each other.
   B. In order to keep friendship, true friends need meet up often.
   C. True friends can be regarded as family members.
   D. Less correspondence will do harm to friendship.
2. What effect does geographical separation bring to friendship? _____
   A. It will do harm to true friendship.
   B. True friendship won't thrive.
   C. True friendship will fade away.
   D. It won't affect true friendship.
3. Which of the following words has similar meaning with "desert" in paragraph 4? _____
   A. abandon   B. oppose   C. criticize   D. affect
4. What do friends react to each other's differences? _____
   A. Best friends analyze each other's differences.
   B. Best friends hide each other's differences.
   C. Best friends don't stand each other's differences.
   D. Best friends accept each other's differences.
5. Which of the following is correct about friends and best friends? _____
   A. All best friends are friends, and all friends can be best friends.

B. Not all best friends are friends, but all friends can be best friends.

C. All best friends are friends, but not all friends can be best friends.

D. Not all best friends are friends, and not all friends can be best friends.

Part Four   Exercises

Task 1   Choose the definition from Column B that best matches each word or phrase in Column A.

A	B
1. comfort	a. having the quality of something good and pleasant
2. resistance	b. to put up with something or somebody unpleasant
3. thrive	c. to keep in a certain state, position, or activity
4. essence	d. a state of being relaxed and feeling no pain
5. maintain	e. the quality of being similar
6. positive	f. to grow stronger
7. affect	g. the most basic and important quality of something
8. constant	h. the action of opposing something
9. similarity	i. to have an effect upon
10. endure	j. happening regularly or all the time

Task 2   Fill in the blanks with the words or expressions given below. Change the form where necessary.

| oppose | analyze | comfort | wonder | maintain |
| affect | similarity | constant | positive | comment |

1. He spoke a few words of _____ to me before leaving.
2. He has a _____ attitude towards life.
3. The two boys look very _____ .
4. I won't _____ on what people say.
5. The teacher tried to _____ the cause of our failure.
6. Mankind have been trying every means to _____ the balance of nature.
7. He _____ writes articles for the local paper.
8. They _____ the government's new policies.
9. I _____ whether you like her.
10. The amount of rain _____ the growth of crops.

Task 3 Translate the following sentences into English, paying special attention to the underlined parts.

1. 语言的本质是沟通。(essence)
2. 客机逐渐消失在雾中。(faded away)
3. 他被看作我们的好朋友之一。(is counted as)
4. 他所有的朋友都抛弃了他!(desert)
5. 我再也不能忍受她的无礼了。(endure)

Part Five Supplementary Reading

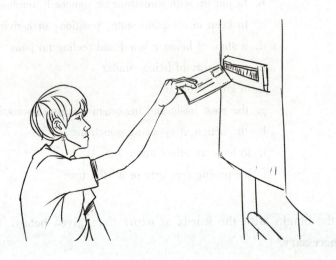

Pen Friends

  Pen friend, also known popularly as pen pals, is quite a popular way to make new friends. Pen friendship is developed when people write to each other regularly through postal mail. It was a popular means of making friends in different parts of the world before internet came into being. Pen pals are more or less like e-friends. Mostly, pen friendship aims at learning other cultures, different lifestyles and to even get rid of loneliness. Some pen friends write each other regularly and in due time also meet. Others remain pen friends forever, exchanging letters and gifts every now and then but never meet. Some pen pals eventually lose touch and their friendship doesn't last long. In case you are unaware about how to make pen pals, read on.

How to Make a Pen Friend

  The easiest way to make pen pals is by joining a pen pal friendship club. There are many such clubs that offer pen friendship all over the world. You can choose your own age group, occupations, hobby, likes and dislikes or even choose someone from a totally different environment and culture. You can gain much broader understanding of the world and numerous cultures by joining a pen pal network.

To save time and energy, pen pals these days exchange letters and cards over the internet. It not only saves time but also money and energy. It makes conversation much more immediate and fast. One doesn't have to wait forever for the traditional snail mail to arrive. It is the newest way to make friends.

Tips for Making Pen Pals

• Do not make pen pals casually. Choose friends according to your hobbies, occupation, and culture.

• Do not give your personal address; you can post letters through mail box numbers, which you can get in any post office.

• Do not reveal very personal information in the initial stages of friendship. Restrict your friendship to the professional front only.

• Decide a fix interval for posting a letter to your pen pal.

• Do not accept the proposal of meeting very early. In case you can't wait to meet take some trustworthy person along with you.

• Do not send your or your family members' photographs in the very beginning of your friendship.

• Do not disclose your financial details specially the PIN number of your ATM or bank account details.

• If you feel that he/she is not the right person to be in touch with you can always stop replying and disconnect all the contacts.

(This text is adapted from *http: //festionals iloueindia.com*, 2011-12-15.)

New Words

pal	[pæl]	n.	a close friend 朋友，伙伴
postal	[ˈpəustəl]	adj.	of or relating to the system for delivering mail 邮政的
due	[djuː]	adj.	scheduled to arrive, suitable to or expected in the circumstances 到期的，应有的；适当的，正当的
remain	[riˈmein]	v.	to stay the same; to keep in a certain state 保持
exchange	[iksˈtʃeindʒ]	v.	to give and receive (information, ideas, etc) 交换
club	[klʌb]	n.	a formal association of people with similar interests 社团，俱乐部
occupation	[ˌɔkjuˈpeiʃən]	n.	a job or profession 职业

immediate	[iˈmiːdiət]	adj.	happening or done at once and without delay 立即的，直接的
snail mail			the system of sending letters by post 蜗牛邮件（指通过邮局邮递的邮件）
casually	[ˈkæʒjuəli]	adv.	not methodically or according to plan 任意地，随便地，胡乱地
personal	[ˈpɜːsənəl]	adj.	of or relating to the private aspects of a person's life 个人的，私人的
reveal	[riˈviːl]	vt.	to make known something that was previously secret or unknown 显示，透露
initial	[iˈniʃəl]	adj.	occurring at the beginning 开始的，最初的
interval	[ˈintəvəl]	n.	a period of time between two events 间隔，间歇
proposal	[prəˈpəuzl]	n.	a plan or suggestion 提议，建议
disclose	[disˈkləuz]	vt.	to make something publicly known 揭露
financial	[faiˈnænʃəl]	adj.	relating to money or the management of money 金融的，财政的
PIN	[pin]		personal identification number 个人标识号
account	[əˈkaunt]	n.	arrangement in which a bank keeps your money safe so that you can pay more in or take money out 账，账户
contact	[ˈkɔntækt]	n.	communication with a person, organization, country etc. 联系，联络，交往

Phrases & Expressions

according to: in a way that depends on differences in situations or amounts 根据，依照
例: He varies the treatment according to circumstances. 他根据情况，变换治疗方法。

Comprehension of the Text

Answer the following questions according to the text.

1. What is the purpose of making pen friends?
2. What is the easiest way to make pen friends?
3. How do you choose pen friends?

Part Six　Grammar

冠词（Articles）

冠词本身不能单独使用，也没有词义，它用在名词的前面，帮助指明名词的含义。英语中的冠词有三种，一种是定冠词，另一种是不定冠词，还有一种是零冠词。

一、不定冠词的用法

不定冠词 a（an）与数词 one 同源，是"一个"的意思。a 用于辅音音素前，一般读作 /ə/，而 an 则用于元音音素前，一般读作 /ən/。a（an）主要有如下用法：

（1）表示"一个"，意为 one；指某人或某物，意为 a certain。例如：

A Mr. Wang called you ten minutes ago. 十分钟以前有位王先生打电话找你。

（2）代表一类人或物。例如：

A friend in need is a friend indeed. 患难朋友才是真正的朋友。

（3）组成词组或成语，如 a little，a few，a lot，a type of，a pile，a great many，many a，as a rule，in a hurry，in a minute，in a word，in a short while，after a while，have a cold，have a try，keep an eye on，all of a sudden 等。

二、定冠词的用法

定冠词 the 与指示代词 this，that 同源，有"那（这）个"的意思，但意义较弱，可以和一个名词连用，来表示某个或某些特定的人或物。the 主要有如下用法。

（1）特指双方都明白的人或物。例如：

Take the umbrella. 带上伞。

（2）指上文提到过的人或事。例如：

He bought a new bike. I've seen the bike. 他买了新自行车。我见过那辆车。

（3）指世上独一无二的事物，如 the sun，the sky，the moon，the earth 等。

（4）与单数名词连用表示一类事物。例如：

the dollar 美元　　　the fox 狐狸

与形容词或分词连用，表示一类人。例如：

the old 老人　　　the poor 穷人

（5）用在序数词和形容词最高级，以及形容词 only，very，same 等前面。例如：

—Where do you live? 你住在哪儿？

—I live on the sixth floor. 我住在六层。

He is the very person I've been looking for. 他就是我要找的人。

（6）与复数名词连用，指整个群体。例如：

They are the students of this school.（指全体学生）

They are students of this school.（指部分学生）

（7）表示所有，相当于物主代词，用在表示身体部位的名词前。例如：

He hit me in the face. 他打我的脸了。

（8）用在某些由普通名词构成的国家名称、机关团体、阶级等专有名词前。例如：

the People's Republic of China 中华人民共和国

the United States 美国

（9）用在表示乐器的名词之前。例如：

My daughter can play the piano. 我女儿会弹钢琴。

（10）用在姓氏的复数名词之前，表示一家人。例如：

the Smiths 史密斯一家人（或史密斯夫妇）

（11）用在惯用语中。例如：

in the day, in the morning (afternoon, evening), the day after tomorrow, the day before yesterday, the next morning, in the sky (water, field, country), in the dark, in the rain, in the distance, in the middle (of), in the end, on the whole, by the way, go to the theatre 等。

三、零冠词的用法

零冠词主要有如下用法：

（1）国名、人名前通常不用定冠词，如 England, Mary。

（2）泛指的复数名词，表示一类人或事物时，可不用定冠词。例如：

They are migrant workers. 他们是民工。

（3）抽象名词表示一般概念时，通常不加冠词。例如：

Failure is the mother of success. 失败乃成功之母。

（4）物质名词表示一般概念时，通常不加冠词。例如：

Fish can not live without water. 鱼儿离不开水。

（5）在季节、月份、节日、假日、日期、星期等表示时间的名词之前，不加冠词。例如：

We have classes from Monday to Friday. 我们从星期一到星期五都上课。

（6）在称呼或表示官衔、职位的名词前不加冠词。例如：

President Obama is addressing the whole nation. 奥巴马总统在对全国人民讲话。

（7）在三餐、球类运动和娱乐运动的名称前，不加冠词，如 have breakfast, play chess。

（8）当两个或两个以上名词并用时，常省去冠词。例如：

I can't write a letter without pen or pencil. 没有钢笔或铅笔，我就写不了信。

（9）当 by 与火车等交通工具连用，表示一种方式时，中间无冠词，如 by bus, by train。

（10）有些个体名词不用冠词，如 school, college, prison, market, hospital, bed, table, class, town, church, court 等，直接置于介词后，表示该名词的深层含义。例如：

go to hospital 去医院看病

go to the hospital 去医院（并不是去看病，而是有其他目的）

（11）序数词前不用冠词的情况：

①序数词前有物主代词时。

②序数词作副词。例如：

He came first in the running competition. 他跑步得了第一。

③在固定词组中，如 at（the）first, first of all, from first to last 等。

四、冠词与形容词+名词结构

（1）两个形容词都有冠词，表示两个不同的人或物。例如：

a black and a white cat 一只黑猫和一只白猫

the black and the white cats 这只黑猫和这只白猫

（2）如果后一个形容词无冠词，则指一人或一物。例如：

a black and white cat 一只花猫

五、冠词位置

1. 不定冠词的位置

不定冠词常位于名词或名词修饰语前，但要注意下面几点：

（1）不定冠词通常位于 such，what，many，half 等形容词之后。例如：

such a long tail 那么长的一个尾巴

Many a man are turning up on the street. 许多人出现在街道上。

（2）当名词前的形容词被副词 as，so，too，how，however，enough 修饰时，不定冠词应放在形容词之后。例如：

He is as clever a boy as his brother is. 他和他哥哥一样是聪明的孩子。

So clever a boy. 这么聪明的一个孩子。

（3）quite，rather 与单数名词连用，冠词放在其后。但当 rather，quite 后有形容词时，不定冠词放在其前后均可，如 rather a cold day/a rather cold day。

（4）在 as，though 引导的让步状语从句中，当表语为形容词修饰的名词时，不定冠词放在形容词后。例如：

Clever a boy as he is, he does not study well. 他虽然聪明，但学习不好。

2. 定冠词的位置

定冠词通常位于名词或名词修饰语前，但放在 all，both，double，half，twice，three times 等词之后，名词之前。例如：

All the friends offered to help. 所有的朋友都伸出援助之手。

练 习

I. 选择题。

1. When Mary was a child, her grandmother always let her have _____ bed.

   A. the breakfast in   B. the breakfast in the

   C. breakfast in   D. breakfast in the

2. The father has promised to give up _____ hundreds of times.

   A. a tobacco   B. tobacco   C. the tobacco   D. tobaccos

3. _____ usually go to church every Sunday.

   A. The Brown   B. A Brown   C. Browns   D. The Browns

4. The train is running fifty miles _____.

A. an hour   B. one hour   C. the hour   D. a hour

5. He can play almost every kind of music instrument but he is good _____.

   A. at the flute   B. at flute   C. at a flute   D. at that flute

6. The investigators found that more should be done for _____ in India.

   A. those poor   B. a poor   C. poor   D. the poor

7. You look in high spirit. You must have _____ during your holiday.

   A. wonderful time   B. a wonderful time
   C. the wonderful time   D. some wonderful time

8. The city assigned a policeman to the school crossing because _____ traffic there was so heavy.

   A. a   B. an   C. the   D. one

9. A new teacher was sent to the village in place of _____ one who had retired.

   A. a   B. the   C. an   D. its

10. Virtue and vice are before you; _____ leads you to happiness, _____ to misery.

    A. the former…latter   B. a former…a latter
    C. the former…the latter   D. former…latter

11. The children in the kindergarden soon took _____ to their teachers.

    A. quite fancy   B. a quite fancy
    C. quite a fancy   D. the quite fancy

12. _____ tend to bemoan the lack of character in the young generation.

    A. The old   B. Old   C. Elderly   D. Older

13. A man suffering from a choke should be given _____.

    A. hot sweet tea   B. a hot sweet tea
    C. the hot sweet tea   D. one hot sweet tea

14. He answered my questions with _____ not to be expected of an ordinary schoolboy.

    A. his accuracy   B. a accuracy
    C. the accuracy   D. an accuracy

15. If you go by train you can have quite _____ comfortable journey.

    A. the   B. one   C. a   D. that

16. We're going to _____ with _____ today, aren't we?

    A. the tea…the Smiths   B. tea…those Smiths
    C. a tea…a Smith   D. tea…the Smiths

17. I want an assistant with _____ knowledge of French and _____ experience of office routine.

    A. the…the   B. a…the   C. a…an   D. the…an

18. Linda's habit of riding a motorcycle up and down the road early in the morning annoyed the neighbors and _____ they took her to the court.

    A. in the end   B. at the end   C. in an end   D. in end

19. It is reported that today _____ president will have lunch with _____ President

Obama.

    A. the...the   B. a...a   C. the.../   D. /.../

20. Tian'anmen Square and _____ Great Wall are two of the places everyone should see in _____ People's Republic of China.

    A. the...the   B. /.../   C. the.../   D. /...the

Ⅱ．用合适的冠词填空。

1. If you come _____ second in the race, you'll get _____ qualification to compete for the next round.

2. We had _____ nice dinner after the meeting with _____ dishes of fish, meat, vegetables and dessert.

3. While income worry is _____ rather common problem of the aged, loneliness is another problem that _____ aged parents may face.

4. Obama has been elected _____ first black president of the United States, and the interactional society expects to have _____ new USA under his leadership.

5. *The New York Times* started _____ new text messaging service that delivers _____ latest news to mobile phones.

6. — My flight was delayed because of _____ heavy rain.

    — But you are just in _____ time for the discussion.

7. Would you like _____ knife and fork? Or would you like to use _____ chopsticks, sir?

8. Have you heard _____ news? The price of _____ petrol around the world is going up by 50%!

9. In the United States, there is always _____ flow of people to areas of _____ country where more jobs can be found.

10. _____ apple fell from the tree and hit him on _____ head.

Part Seven   Writing

Schedule

Directions: In this part, you are going to learn how to write a *Schedule* and then try your hand.

1. Read the following sample.

    Wang Mei's Week Schedule for Her Free Time

Sept. 6 Monday	2:00 p.m. 7:00 p.m.	go to the library attend a lecture on elective courses
Sept. 7 Tuesday	3:00 p.m. 4:00 p.m.	visit the labs at college attend a Students' Union activity
Sept. 8 Wednesday	2:00 p.m. 8:00 p.m.	go to the gym do math homework
Sept. 9 Thursday	2:00 p.m. 4:00 p.m.	visit Professor Song watch TV program on Teachers' Day
Sept. 10 Friday	2:00 p.m. 7:00 p.m.	play table tennis communicate with friends online
Sept. 11 Saturday	8:00 a.m. 2:00 p.m. 7:30 p.m.	go shopping downtown visit the Science Museum see a film with classmates
Sept. 12 Sunday	9:00 a.m. 4:00 p.m.	take part in Art Training in Students' Center attend a class meeting

2. Translate the following schedule into English.

杨刚的一周业余时间安排

9月13日 星期一	下午2:00 参加学生会活动 晚7:30 听美国文学讲座
9月14日 星期二	下午2:00 去图书馆 晚7:00 班会
9月15日 星期三	下午4:00 打篮球 晚7:00 上网和家人联系
9月16日 星期四	下午3:30 拜访王教授 晚7:00 做数学作业
9月17日 星期五	下午4:00 参加篮球比赛 晚7:00 和同学去看电影
9月18日 星期六	上午9:00 参观十三陵 下午2:00 游览长城
9月19日 星期日	上午9:00 洗衣服 下午3:00 看足球比赛

Data Bank

attend a lecture on   参加……讲座
Students' Union   学生会

Unit 4

Students' Center	学生活动中心
Teachers' Day	教师节
the Science Museum	科技馆
math homework	数学作业
chemistry lab	化学实验室
gym (gymnasium)	体育馆
sports ground	运动场
basketball games	篮球比赛
volleyball	排球
badminton	羽毛球
communicate with family online	上网和家人联系
the Forbidden City	故宫
Ming Tombs	(明) 十三陵
Summer Palace	颐和园
the Temple of Heaven	天坛

Tips

在英语中，用来标明具体时刻的缩写 a. m. 和 p. m. 源自拉丁语，是拉丁语 ante meridiem（在正午之前）和 post meridiem（在正午之后）的缩写形式。所以，在英语时间表中，晚上午夜之前的时刻缩写用 p. m. 来表示，而午夜后至正午前的时刻缩写用 a. m. 来表示。

69

Test Paper 1

Part I Listening Comprehension (15 minutes)

Directions: This part is to test your listening ability. It consists of 3 sections.

Section A

Directions: This section is to test your ability to give proper answers to questions. There are 5 recorded questions in it. After each question, there is a pause. The questions will be spoken two times. When you hear a question, you should decide on the correct answer from the 4 choices marked A), B), C) and D) given in your test paper. Then you should mark the corresponding letter on the Answer Sheet with a single line through the centre.

Example:
You will hear: I wonder if you could give Mr. Wang a message for me?
You will read: A) I'm not sure.
                 B) You're right.
                 C) Yes, certainly.
                 D) That's interesting.

From the question we learn that the speaker is asking the listener to leave a message. Therefore, "C) Yes, certainly" is the correct answer. You should mark C) on the Answer Sheet. Now the test will begin.

1. A) Yes, I did.   B) No, I didn't.
   C) It was a waste of time.   D) It lasts two hours.
2. A) It's over there.   B) It's 9:30.
   C) It's too late.   D) It sounds good.
3. A) No, that's not good.   B) Yes, it is.
   C) It doesn't matter.   D) So do I.
4. A) Yes, I look pale.   B) I've got a head ache.
   C) Nor am I.   D) Don't mention it.
5. A) I'm looking for a gift for my wife.   B) You can do it right now.
   C) I'd rather not.   D) Thank you very much.

Section B

Directions: This section is to test your ability to understand short dialogues. There are 5 recorded dialogues in it. After each dialogue, there is a recorded question. The dialogues and questions will be spoken two times. When you hear a question, you should decide on the correct answer from the 4 choices marked A), B), C) and D) given in your test paper. Then you should mark the corresponding letter on the Answer Sheet with a single line through the centre.

6. A) She didn't know the time.   B) She forgot her class.
   C) She didn't catch the bus.   D) The bus was late.
7. A) 9:00.   B) 9:50.
   C) 8:45.   D) 8:15.
8. A) In a store.   B) On a plane.   C) In the hospital.   D) At the theatre.
9. A) Vegetables.   B) Clothes.   C) Fruit.   D) Books.
10. A) Jason Daniel isn't at home right how.
    B) Jason Daniel doesn't want to answer the phone.
    C) The man can call back later.
    D) The man got the wrong number.

Section C

Directions: In this section you will hear a short recorded passage. The passage is printed in the test paper, but with some words or phrases missing. The passage will be read three times. During the second reading, you are required to put the missing words or phrases that you hear on the Answer Sheet in order of the numbered blanks. The third reading is for you to check your writing. Now the passage will begin.

Since World War Ⅱ, especially in the last few decades of the 20th century, large groups of foreigners have come and settled in the United States. The (11) _____ is that many Americans speak a foreign language at home. Today, one in seven Americans speaks a language (12) _____ English. Spanish is the leading foreign language spoken by 17 million Americans. 31.8 million Americans speak 329 foreign languages in the (13) _____. That means there is an increase of 34 percent in foreign language usage since 1980. Asian languages are used by 14 percent of foreign language speakers. That (14) _____ the new wave of immigrants from Asian countries (15) _____ India, Japan, Korea and the Philippines. However, fewer European languages are heard in American families than before.

11. _____
12. _____
13. _____
14. _____
15. _____

Part II Vocabulary & Structure (15 minutes)

Directions: This part is to test your ability to use words and phrases to construct meaningful and grammatically correct sentences. It consists of 2 sections.

Section A

Directions: There are 10 incomplete statements here. You are required to complete each statement by choosing the appropriate answer from the 4 choices marked A), B), C) and D). You should mark the corresponding letter on the Answer Sheet with a single line through the centre.

16. One of my foreign friends is looking forward to _____ my country.
    A) visit　　　　B) visiting　　　　C) having visited　　　　D) be visiting

17. This car has been nothing _____ trouble — it's always breaking down.
    A) only　　　　B) merely　　　　C) simply　　　　D) but

18. Not until I began to work _____ how much time I had wasted.
    A) have I realized　　B) I have realized　　C) did I realize　　D) I realized

19. If I can manage, I feel like _____ some running no matter how busy I am.
    A) do　　　　B) to　　　　C) doing　　　　D) done

20. If you think twice _____ you speak, you will speak twice better for it.
    A) after　　　　B) when　　　　C) as　　　　D) before

21. The computer will run the program for you when you _____ the button.
    A) will press　　B) press　　C) would press　　D) pressed

22. The chair looks rather hard but actually it is very comfortable to sit _____ .
    A) at　　　　B) on　　　　C) over　　　　D) under

23. This is one of the longest bridges that _____ on this river.
    A) is ever built　　　　　　　　B) has ever been built
    C) was ever built　　　　　　　D) has ever built

24. Oh, Jenny, I really appreciate _____ to see me off. You are so thoughtful.
    A) you to come　　B) that you come　　C) your coming　　D) that you came

25. He suddenly left for Paris yesterday; _____ was more than we had expected.
    A) that　　　　B) what　　　　C) which　　　　D) this

Section B

Directions: There are also 10 incomplete statements here. You should fill in each blank with the proper form of the word given in the brackets. Write the word or words in the corresponding space on the Answer Sheet.

26. I didn't see your boss at the meeting. If he (come) _____ , I would have told him the news.
27. I have been busy (prepare) _____ for the examination.
28. It is advised that we (choose) _____ a major fit for ourselves.
29. I sincerely thank you for your (invite) _____ to the party.
30. That was the most (attract) _____ program they could think of.
31. I was (please) _____ to have received your letter dated May 20th last month.

32. He rushed (danger) _____ across the busy street to catch the bus.
33. I am (terrible) _____ sorry to learn that you have made no improvement on the design.
34. I'm afraid you have been speaking too fast to make yourself (understand) _____.
35. The machine does not seem to work properly. I think it needs (repair) _____.

Part III Reading Comprehension (40 minutes)

Directions: This part is to test your reading ability. There are 5 tasks for you to fulfill. You should read the reading materials carefully and do the tasks as you are instructed.

Task 1

Directions: After reading the following passage, you will find 5 questions or unfinished statements, numbered 36 through 40. For each question or statement there are 4 choices marked A), B), C) and D). You should make the correct choice and mark the corresponding letter on the Answer Sheet with a single line through the centre.

The sense of sound is one of our most important means of knowing what is going on around us. Sound has a wasted product, too, in the form of noise. Noise has been called unwanted sound. Noise is growing and may get much worse before it get any better.

Scientists, for several years, have been studying how noise affects people and animals. They are surprised by what they have learned. Peace and quiet are becoming harder to find. Noise pollution is a threat that should be looked at carefully.

There is a saying about it being so noisy that you can't hear yourself think. Doctors who study noise believe that we must sometimes hear ourselves think. If we don't we may have headaches, other aches and pains, or even worse mental problems.

Noise adds more tension (紧张) to a society that already faces enough stress.

But noise is not a new problem. In ancient Rome, people complained so much about noise that the government stopped chariots (四轮马车) from moving through the streets at night!

Ways of making less noise are now being tested. There are even laws controlling noise. We can not return to the "good old days" of peace and quiet. But we can reduce noise—if we shout loudly enough about it.

36. Why are scientists surprised by the findings in their noise study?
   A) Because the world is becoming more and more noisy.
   B) Because they have learned that noise is also a kind of pollution.
   C) Because noise is an unwanted waste for human beings.
   D) Because people knew little about the danger of noise before.

37. What may be the result if we can not hear ourselves think?
   A) We may forget what we have thought about.
   B) Our thoughts may be interfered.
   C) Our mind may be harmed.
   D) We may have difficulty using the right words.

38. When the writer says we can not return to the good old days, he means that _____.

A) our society is becoming much worse than before

B) in our modern society it is hard to lead a quiet life

C) the old days were much happier than the present time

D) it is impossible for us to deal with noise as we did before

39. From the last sentence of the passage we can learn that _____.

A) we can put noise under control if our measures are effective

B) sometimes we have to shout loudly so that others can hear us

C) shouting is a chief cause of noise pollution

D) it is important to warn people of the danger of noise pollution

40. Which of the following is TRUE according to the passage?

A) Only recently did people realize the harmfulness of noise.

B) Noise pollution is the worst kind of pollution we suffer from.

C) People are now trying to find ways to make noise as low as possible.

D) The writer thinks that it is almost impossible for people to avoid noise.

Task 2

Directions: This task is the same as Task 1. The 5 questions or unfinished statements are numbered 41 through 45.

A budget (预算) is a spending plan. It can help you spend money wisely. It can do this by cutting out wasteful spending. Of course, preparing a budget takes planning, and following a budget takes willpower (自制力). Your budget should meet your family's needs and income.

The first step in creating a budget is to set your goals. What does your family need and want? You must know this to work out the details of the budget. Keep goals realistic, in terms of income available. Then decide which goals are the most important.

The next step is estimating family income. Before you can plan wisely, you need to know how much money you have to spend! Write down all the money you expect to receive (wages, savings, interest, etc.) during the planned budget period.

After you have calculated how much money will be available, it is time to estimate expenses (消费). List all of your family expenses.

If you are not satisfied with what you got for your money, look carefully at your spending. Studying your records will show where overspending has occurred. It will also point out poor buying habits.

It is also a good idea to set aside a small amount of money for emergencies. Every family has small emergencies: a blown tire, a broken device, or the need for minor medical care.

41. According to the passage, what is the advantage of a budget?

A) It can help you set your goals clearly.

B) It can help you save a lot of money.

C) It can help you get rid of poor buying habits.

D) It can help you spend money in a reasonable way.

42. In carrying out your budget, you need _____.

A) to have the ability to control yourself

B) to ask your family members for advice

C) to cut it down as much as possible

D) to take care not to buy expensive things

43. One advantage of keeping a record of your spending is that _____.

    A) you will remember how much you have already spent

    B) you will know if you have spent more money than you planned

    C) you will be able to tell your family what should not be bought

    D) you will learn how to make a better budget next time

44. The writer suggests that it is a good idea to set aside some money because _____.

    A) you probably will not be able to follow your budget

    B) people usually spend more than they plan to do

    C) things can happen unexpectedly

    D) others may want to borrow some money from you

45. This passage is mainly about _____.

    A) the meaning of a budget

    B) the relation between budget and income

    C) the way a budget is made

    D) the importance of making a budget

Task 3

Directions: The following is an advertisement by a travel service. After reading it, you should fill in the blanks marked 46 through 50 in the table below.

Whether you're looking for a quiet place or a holiday trip, Florida's natural beauty and various tourist activities let you make your dream alive. Nature lovers can explore hundreds of acres (英亩) of lakes, forests and wetlands filled with native birds, fish and wildlife (野生动物).

Florida is a sportsman's paradise (乐园) as well, with plenty of opportunities for water sports lovers, and Florida is also the nation's best tennis place, with over 7,700 tennis facilities. With thousands of rivers and lakes, plus over 1,000 miles of beaches on the Atlantic Ocean and Gulf (海湾) of Mexico, Florida is a water sports wonder land. Florida is also home to some of the best attractions in the United States, from technologically advanced parks to historic museums.

Welcome to Florida, ladies and gentlemen!

Florida is most attractive because of

1. its (46) _____, and

2. its (47) _____.

Visitors to Florida are mainly

1. (48) _____ and

2. sportsmen.

Among the various sports Florida offers, the most wonderful are (49) _____.

Florida has a beach as long as (50) _____ miles.

Task 4

Directions: Read the following passage. After reading it, you are required to complete the statements (numbered 51 through 55) below it. You should write your answers briefly on the Answer Sheet correspondingly.

Job-hunting Myths

Don't defeat yourself by accepting common myths, says the head of an international consulting (咨询) company.

Myth 1: If there's nothing available in your field, switch careers.

Fact 1: That's one of the worst things you can do. You compete against others with experience, and you will not approach your old salary level.

Myth 2: Lower your salary demands. You'll be more attractive to employers in an uncertain economy.

Fact 2: People who ask for less are viewed as "undesirable property". If you are considered anything less than first class, you are not likely to be hired.

Myth 3: If you are over 50, it will be very hard to find another job.

Fact 3: Workers over 50 win new jobs almost as quickly as youngsters do. Today's employers place a premium (额外补贴) on experience.

Myth 4: Bring up salary as quickly as possible in the first interview.

Fact 4: That's fast way to be removed (取消) from consideration. It tells employers you are more concerned with yourself than with the company.

Myth 5: You can only get interviews between 9 a.m. and 5 p.m. on weekdays.

Fact 5: Employers are often available before and after regular hours when the office is quieter. If you get an interview then, you've got an employer's concentrated attention.

51. What is the disadvantage of changing your career?

    You will not reach _____.

52. What will be the result if you are not considered as first class?

    You are less possible to _____.

53. What actually will experienced older people get?

    They are likely to get _____.

54. What will happen if you ask for a high salary in the first interview?

    It will make you _____ the job.

55. What is a better time for an interview?

    Not _____.

Part IV   Translation—English to Chinese（15 minutes）

Directions：This part is to test your ability to translate English into Chinese. There are 4 sentences（numbered 56 through 59）, and two short paragraphs（No. 60）in this part. Write your translation in the corresponding space on the Answer Sheet.

56. A busy shopping centre is usually also a good location for a restaurant.

57. Customers prefer to purchase our products though they seem higher in price.

58. I have to come to discuss with you about the measures we shall take to cope with the situation.

59. If you can provide satisfactory after sale service, your products will surely have a wide market here.

60. A) In the following days Jack was immersed in great happiness. He called his parents to express his gratitude（感激）for their wonderful encouragement and his teachers to express his appreciation for their marvelous（巨大的）support. By doing so he shared his success with his relations（家人）and friends rather than enjoying it all by himself.

B) Dear Customer,

In this month's newsletter（通讯）, you'll find an interesting and useful topic（主题）: Gardening（园艺）.

It's really true that gardens can not only add beauty but also value to your home. Many experts recommend gardening as a way to relax and reduce stress. April is the perfect time to start planning a new garden.

Part V   Writing（15 minutes）

Directions：This part is to test your ability to do practical writing. You are required to write a business card according to the following instructions.

Mr. Zhang Liang is the Personnel Manager of the Legend Co. Ltd. His address is Personnel Department, 18th floor, Trade Center Building, 15 Kunshan Road, Shanghai; Post Code: 200808; Email: zhliang@163.com; Tel: 021-85857676, and Mobile: 13901234567. Design a business card for him.

Unit 5

Romance

Part One Warm-up

1. Think of terms related to romance and put them in the following box.

2. Do you think romance is important in your love life?
3. Is dating a very common scene at your college now? What do you think of it?
4. Would you like to describe what kind of sweetheart do you want to find?

Unit 5

 Part Two Speaking and Listening

Section A   Listen to the following conversation and then repeat.

Man: Do you love me?
Women: I'm very fond of you.
Man: Yes, but do you love me?
Woman: Uh... You mean a lot to me.
Man: Why won't you answer my question?
Woman: What question?
Man: Do you love me? Come on! I want to know.
Woman: I care for you very deeply. You know that.
Man: That isn't the same thing!
Woman: What kind of answer do you expect?
Man: The truth! I want the truth!
Woman: How can I possibly answer such a question?

Section B   Listen to the following short passage and fill in the missing words.

It is true that some people fall in love at first 1) _____ . If the first meeting leaves a good impression on each other and both sides are 2) _____ by the other's way of talking and 3) _____ , we can say they have a good beginning for a love story. If they date for a couple of times, they may be madly in love.

However, things may not always go as well as 4) _____ . Although the first sight leave a good impression, he or she may find that the person is not right for him or her after one knows the other well. Then, it is 5) _____ for her/him to stop this love when it just begins.

79

Part Three Detailed Reading

Two Kellys, One Match

Kelly Hildebrandt is not going to worry about whether or not to take her future husband's name. It is not important now. This October, the 20-year-old girl will vow to share her life with a man whose name she already shares. And it's not only a surname that links the two. Florida student Kelly Katrina Hildebrandt, 20, is to marry a fellow Kelly Hildebrandt, a 24-year-old financial services worker, Kelly Carl Hildebrandt.

The two have planned a wedding for 100 guests to witness them become husband and wife. "He is just everything that I've ever looked for," Miss Hildebrand said of her fiancé. "A good guy must have certain qualities. And he has all the ones I could think of and more."

Their modern romance was a match made in cyberspace. Bored and curious one night last year, she typed her name into the search bar on popular social networking website Facebook just to see if anyone shared it. At the time, Kelly Hildebrandt, a Texas boy, was the only match, so she sent him a message. "She said: 'Hi. We have the same name. I think it is cool,'" Kelly Carl Hildebrandt recalled. "I thought she was pretty cute." But there were also concerns. "I thought, we've got to be related or something," said Mr. Hildebrandt.

For the next three months the two exchanged emails. Before long, occasional phone calls turned into daily chats, sometimes lasting hours. Mr. Hildebrandt visited his namesake in Florida after a few months and fell in love with the girl from head to heel. "I thought it was fun," he said of that first online encounter. "I had no idea that it would lead to this."

Months after Kelly sent her first email, she found a diamond engagement ring hidden in a treasure box on a beach in December. "I totally think that it's all God's timing," she said. "He planned it out just perfect."

It hasn't been all plain sailing since then, but some trouble did come along with their similar names. Once, their romantic trip on a cruise ship almost got cancelled when the travel agent deleted one ticket from the system, thinking someone had entered the same information twice.

The two were also uncertain about how to write their wedding invitations, so they decided to include their middle names. Miss Hildebrandt says there are no plans to pass along the name to their future children. "No," she said. "We're definitely not going to name our kids Kelly."

(This text is adapted from http://www.dailymail.co.uk, 2011-11-08.)

New Words

vow	[vau]	v.	to promise solemnly 发誓，庄严地承诺
surname	[ˈsəːneim]	n.	a name shared in common to identify the members of a family 姓
Florida	[ˈflɔridə]	n.	佛罗里达（美国的一个州）
Kelly	[ˈkeli]	n.	凯莉（人名）
Hildebrandt	[ˈhildəbrænt]	n.	希尔德布兰德（人名）
wedding	[ˈwediŋ]	n.	the ceremony or celebration of a marriage 婚礼
witness	[ˈwitnis]	vt. & n.	to be present at or have personal knowledge of 出席，见证
fiancé	[fiˈɑːnsei]	n.	〈法〉未婚夫（fiancée 未婚妻）
match	[mætʃ]	n.	one that is like another in one or more specified qualities 相配、般配的人或事物
cyberspace	[ˈsaibəspeis]	n.	a computer network consisting of a worldwide network 网络空间
bore	[bɔː]	v.	to cause to be bored 使厌烦
curious	[ˈkjuəriəs]	adj.	eagerly interested in learning more 好奇的
search bar		n.	搜索栏
Facebook	[ˈfeisbuk]	n.	脸谱网（美国的一个社交网站）
Texas	[ˈteksəs]	n.	德克萨斯（美国的一个州）
recall	[riˈkɔːl]	v.	to recollect knowledge from memory 回忆，回想
cute	[kjuːt]	adj.	lovely 可爱的，聪明的
concern	[kənˈsəːn]	n.	something that interests you because it is important or

			affects you 关心，忧虑，关心的事
		v.	to have to do with or be relevant to 涉及，影响，关心
related	[rɪˈleɪtɪd]	adj.	be in a relationship with 相关的，有关系的，同种的
occasional	[əˈkeɪʒənəl]	adj.	occurring from time to time 偶尔的，不时的
namesake	[ˈneɪmseɪk]	n.	a person with the same name as another 同名人，同名物
encounter	[ɪnˈkaʊntə]	n.	a meeting, especially one that is unplanned or unexpected 碰见，偶然相遇
engagement	[ɪnˈgeɪdʒmənt]	n.	a mutual promise to marry 订婚
treasure	[ˈtreʒə]	n.	a collection of precious things 珠宝，珍品
timing	[ˈtaɪmɪŋ]	n.	the time when something happens 时机，时间的选择和安排
cruise	[kruːz]	n.	an ocean trip taken for pleasure 巡游，巡航
cancel	[ˈkænsl]	v.	to call off; to postpone 取消，撤销
delete	[dɪˈliːt]	v.	to remove; to wipe out 删除
definitely	[ˈdefɪnɪtli]	adv.	without question and beyond doubt 明确地，确切地

Phrases & Expressions

1. **before long**：in the near future 不久以后

   例：Before long our family moved and had to give the pet away. 不久我们搬家了，不得不把宠物送人。

2. **fall in love with**：to have a strong feeling of liking someone a lot combined with sexual attraction 爱上，对……产生爱情

   例：It seems that all the boys have fallen in love with Jenny. 这些男孩好像全都爱上了珍妮。

3. **from head to heel**：over the whole body 从头到脚，完全彻底地

   例：Sophia was trembling from head to heel. 索菲亚浑身都在发抖。

4. **plan out**：design 策划

   例：The engineers are planning out the project. 工程师们正在为那项工程做准备。

5. **plain sailing**：smooth 一帆风顺

   例：From now on it will all be plain sailing. 从现在起，事情就一帆风顺了。

6. **pass along**：hand down 传递；延续

   例：Mothers can pass along their experiences to their daughters. 母亲可以将经验传给她们的女儿们。

Unit 5

Comprehension of the Text

Choose the best answer for each of the following questions.

1. Where did the Miss Kelly Hildebrandt encounter Mr. Kelly Hildebrandt? _____
   A. At the party.
   B. In the library.
   C. On the Internet.
   D. Near the riverbank.

2. What does the word "namesake" in Paragraph 4 mean? _____
   A. Website.
   B. Relatives.
   C. A place where people can meet with each other.
   D. A person with the same name as another.

3. Which place did Mr. Kelly Hildebrandt choose to express his desire to marry? _____
   A. In a financial service.
   B. On a cruise ship.
   C. In a treasure shop.
   D. At the Seaside.

4. Which of the following statements is TRUE according to the text? _____
   A. Miss Kelly Hildebrandt and Mr. Kelly Hildebrandt live in the same city.
   B. Miss Kelly Hildebrandt and Mr. Kelly Hildebrandt used the same ticket on a cruise-ship trip.
   C. One hundred guests will attend the wedding of Miss Kelly Hildebrandt and Mr. Kelly Hildebrandt.
   D. Miss Kelly Hildebrandt received an engagement ring after she sent her first email.

5. Which of the following statements is NOT true according to the text? _____
   A. Miss Kelly Hildebrandt and Mr. Kelly Hildebrandt are going to name their first baby Kelly in memory of their romance.
   B. Miss Kelly Hildebrandt and Mr. Kelly Hildebrandt are going to marry this October.
   C. Miss Kelly Hildebrandt is four years younger than Mr. Kelly Hildebrandt.
   D. Mr. Hildebrandt fell in love with Miss Kelly Hildebrandt when he visited Miss Kelly Hildebrandt for the first time.

Part Four Exercises

Task 1 Choose the definition from Column B that best matches each word in Column A.

A	B
1. match	a. to promise solemnly
2. recall	b. to be present at or have personal knowledge of
3. wedding	c. a meeting unexpected
4. encounter	d. one that is like another in one or more specified qualities
5. vow	e. to remove by crossing out
6. delete	f. a name to identify the members of a family
7. namesake	g. to recollect knowledge from memory
8. surname	h. not habitual
9. witness	i. the ceremony or celebration of a marriage
10. occasional	j. another person who has a same name as someone

Task 2 Fill in the blanks with the words or expressions given below. Change the form where necessary.

confusion	cyberspace	delete	encounter	engagement
occasional	recall	timing	vow	witness

1. He was just walking into the restaurant when we got there. Perfect _____!
2. Well, I _____ that I would never drink again.
3. There was _____ when a man fired shots.
4. It's easy to create a false tale in _____.
5. I pressed the wrong key and _____ my most important letter.
6. I've had a(n) _____ headache.
7. One night the policemen on patrol had a _____ with a gang of thieves.
8. Harry has just told me about his _____ to Mary.
9. The boy was asked to _____ what happened to him that day.
10. The year of 2009 _____ a global financial crisis.

84

Unit 5

Task 3 Translate the following sentences into English, paying special attention to the underlined parts.

1. 约翰与露茜一见钟情。(fall in love with)
2. 我对她的勇气佩服得五体投地。(from head to heel)
3. 他们正在筹划一个网站。(plan out)
4. 一旦设计问题解决了，一切就顺利了。(plain sailing)
5. 你能把我的建议转告她吗？(pass along)

Part Five Supplementary Reading

A Love Letter Is Never Late

A couple have married after they were reunited when a long-lost love letter sent ten years ago was found unopened behind a fireplace.

Steve Smith and Carmen Ruiz-Perez, both 42, walked into the church on Friday following a separation of 16 years.

The pair fell in love and got engaged in their twenties after Carmen moved to England as a foreign student.

But after a year-long relationship the couple drifted apart when she had to move back to France.

A few years later Steve wrote to her in a bid to relight their romance — but Carmen's mother put it on the mantle and it slipped down the back of the fireplace.

It remained there unopened for the next decade until the fireplace was removed for renovations.

Carmen — who had remained single and never forgot the love of her life — was given the letter in which Steve had written:

85

"I hope you are well. I was just writing to ask if you ever married and if you ever still thought of me? It would be great to hear from you. Please get in touch with me if you can. Steve."

Factory supervisor Steve said: "I didn't write much because I guessed she would be married. I never thought it would take ten years to hear back."

Carmen said she was initially too nervous to call as so much time had passed but encouraged herself to call. And they arranged to meet.

They met up in Paris a few days later and have now wed — 17 years after they first fell in love.

Steve said: "When we met again it was like a film. We ran across the airport into each other's arms."

"We met up and fell in love all over again. Within 30 seconds of setting eyes on each other we were kissing."

"Now we're married. I'm just glad the letter did eventually end up where it was supposed to be."

Carmen, who is now living with Steve in Devon, said the wedding was the summit of an "amazing" love story.

She added: "I never got married and now I'm marrying the man I have always loved."

New Words

reunite	[ˌriːjuːˈnait]	v.	to have a reunion; to unite again 重聚，重新结合
fireplace	[ˈfaiəpleis]	n.	an open space for a fire in the wall of a room 壁炉
church	[tʃəːtʃ]	n.	a place for public (especially Christian) worship 教堂
separation	[ˌsepəˈreiʃən]	n.	the act of dividing or disconnecting 分开，离开
engage	[inˈgeidʒ]	v.	to agree to marry 订婚
relight	[ˌriːˈlait]	v.	to light again 重新点燃
mantle	[ˈmæntl]	n.	shelf that projects from wall above fireplace 壁炉台架
renovation	[ˌrenəˈveiʃən]	n.	the act of improving by renewing and restoring 更新；修复
initially	[iˈniʃəli]	adv.	at the beginning 起初，最初
encourage	[inˈkʌridʒ]	vt.	to give hope or courage to somebody 鼓励，鼓舞
summit	[ˈsʌmit]	n.	the highest stage of development 顶点，顶峰
amazing	[əˈmeiziŋ]	adj.	very surprising and causing pleasure or admiration 令人惊奇的

Phrases & Expressions

1. **drift apart**: lose personal contact over time 疏远

   例：After twelve years of marriage, the two people began to drift apart. 经过了十二年的婚姻生

活后，两个人在感情上开始疏远。

2. **get in touch with**：to communicate with somebody, especially by writing to them or telephoning them 和……取得联系

例：I was not able to get in touch with you yesterday. 我昨天无法和你联络上。

Comprehension of the Text

Answer the following questions according to the text.

1. How many years later did they get married after they first fell in love?
2. Where did the letter go after the mother put it on the mantle?
3. How was the letter found?

 Part Six   Grammar

形容词（Adjectives）

形容词（Adjective）是表示人或事物的属性、特征或状态的词。形容词修饰名词，它的基本用法就是为名词提供更多的信息。形容词分为性质形容词和叙述形容词两类。

直接说明事物的性质或特征的形容词是性质形容词，它有级的变化，可以用程度副词修饰，在句中可作定语、表语和补语。如 hot（热的），friendly（友好的）。

叙述形容词只能作表语，所以又称为表语形容词。这类形容词没有级的变化，也不可用程度副词修饰。大多数以 a 开头的形容词都属于这一类，如 afraid（害怕的）。

请比较下面几个例子：

（错）He is an ill man.

（对）The man is ill.

（错）She is an afraid girl.

（对）The girl is afraid.

类似用法的形容词还有：well, unwell, faint, alike, alive, alone, asleep, awake 等。

一、形容词的判断方法

1. 结构特点

以-able，-al，-ful，-ic，-ish，-less，-ous，-y 等后缀结尾的词，一般是形容词，如 capable（有能力的），mental（心理上的），helpful（有帮助的），atomic（原子的），foolish（愚蠢的），careless（粗心的），curious（好奇的），healthy（健康的），sunny（晴朗的）等。

2. 句法特点

形容词的句法特点有：大多数形容词都可以作定语；在 be, look, seem 等词之后作表语；可用 very 来修饰；有比较级和最高级形式。其中，在句中作定语或作表语是形容词最主要的特点。例如：

She is very pretty. 她很漂亮。（表语）

She is a pretty girl. 她是个漂亮的女孩。（定语）

He was asleep. 他睡着了。（表语）

She is a kind teacher. 她是位和气的老师。（定语）

二、形容词的用法

（1）用作定语。例如：

Cindy is a hardworking student. 辛迪是一个很用功的学生。

（2）用作表语。例如：

The English story is very difficult to understand. 那个英文故事很难懂。

（3）用作宾语补足语。例如：

His child's success made him very happy. 他的孩子的成功让他感到十分高兴。

（4）the+形容词，表示一类人或事物，相当于名词，用作主语及宾语。例如：

The young should always take care of the old. 年轻人总应该照顾年纪大的人。

（5）有时也可用作状语。例如：

He speaks loud and clear. 他讲话声音洪亮且清楚。

（6）少数形容词只能作表语，不能作定语。这类形容词包括 ill, asleep, awake, alone, alive, well, worth, glad, unable, afraid 等。例如：

（对）He is alone. 他是一个人。

（错）He is an alone man.

（对）This place is worth visiting. 这个地方值得参观。

（错）That is a worth place.

（7）少数形容词只能作定语，不能作表语。这些形容词包括 little, live（活着的），elder, eldest 等。例如：

（对）My elder sister went abroad. 我姐姐出国了。

（错）My sister is elder than I.

（对）This is a little house. 这是栋小房子。

（错）The house is little.

三、形容词的位置

1. 形容词的一般位置

形容词一般放在名词前作定语，单个形容词修饰名词时，一般要放在名词的前面。它们的前面常常带有冠词、形容词性代词、指示代词、数词等。例如：

six blind men 六个盲人

my own house 我自己的房子

（1）当形容词所修饰的词是由 some，any，every，no 等构成的不定代词时，形容词必须置于所修饰的词之后。例如：

She has something new to tell me. 她有一些新的情况要告诉我。

（2）形容词后面有介词短语或不定式短语时，形容词必须置于名词之后。例如：

It is a problem difficult to work out. 这是一个难以解决的问题。

（3）在一些特殊用法中，形容词置于所修饰的名词之后。例如：

All people, young or old, should be strict with themselves. 所有的人，无论老少，都应该严格要求自己。

All countries, rich and poor, should help one another. 所有的国家，无论穷富，都应该互相帮助。

（4）有少数形容词，如 enough 和 possible，既可置于所修饰的名词之前，也可置于所修饰的名词之后。例如：

Do you have enough time（time enough）to prepare? 你有足够的时间做准备吗？

Maybe it will be a possible chance（chance possible）for you. 或许它将成为你的一次可能的机遇。

（5）有些形容词，置于名词之前与之后，含义不尽相同。例如：

the singer present 出席的歌手

the present singer 当代的歌手

2. 两个以上的形容词修饰同一个名词时的排列顺序

限定词→一般描绘性形容词→表示大小、长短、高低的形容词→表示形状的形容词→表示年龄、新旧的形容词→表示色彩的形容词→表示国籍、地区、出处的形容词→表示物质、材料的形容词→表示用途、类别的形容词→名词中心词。例如：

an exciting international football match 一场令人激动的国际足球赛

a new red sports shirt 一件新的红色运动衫

a light black plastic umbrella 一把轻的黑塑料伞

a small old brown wooden house 一座小的旧的棕色的木头房子

四、形容词的比较等级

大多数形容词（性质形容词）有比较级和最高级的变化，即原级、比较级和最高级，用来表示事物的等级差别。原级即形容词的原形，比较级和最高级有规则变化和不规则变化两种。

规则变化即单音节词和少数双音节词加词尾 -er, -est 来构成比较级和最高级。规则变化的几种情形详见表 5–1。

表 5-1 比较级和最高级的规则变化

构成法	原级	比较级	最高级
一般单音节词末尾加-er, -est	tall	taller	tallest
以不发音的 e 结尾的单音词和少数以-le 结尾的双音节词只加-r, -st	nice	nicer	nicest
以一个辅音字母结尾的闭音节单音词，双写结尾的辅音字母，再加-er, -est	big	bigger	biggest
以"辅音字母+y"结尾的双音节词，改 y 为 i, 再加-er, -est	busy	busier	busiest
少数以-er, -ow 结尾的双音节词末尾加-er, -est	clever/narrow	cleverer/narrower	cleverest/narrowest
其他双音节词和多音节词，在前面加 more, most 来构成比较级和最高级	important	more important	most important

不规则变化如表 5-2 所示。

表 5-2 比较级和最高级的不规则变化

原级	比较级	最高级
good	better	best
well（健康的）		
bad	worse	worst
ill（有病的）		
old	older/elder	oldest/eldest
much/many	more	most
little	less	least
far	farther/further	farthest/furthest

1. 形容词原级的用法

形容词的原级常用于"as…as"及"not as（so）…as"两种句型中。

句型"as…as"表示两者相比较，程度相同。例如：

The city is as clean as that city. 这座城市与另一座城市一样干净。

句型"not as（so）…as"表示两者相比较，前者不如后者。例如：

I'm not as intelligent as she. 我没有她聪明。

在使用"as…as"与"not as（so）…as"结构时，应该特别注意"as…as"或"not as（so）as…"中间的形容词必须是原级。例如：

Today is as cool as yesterday. 今天与昨天一样凉快。

形容词原级的用法还要注意下面几点。

(1)"数词+times+as+形容词原级+as"（是……的几倍）。例如：

My apples are three times as many as yours. 我的苹果是你的三倍。

(2)"half+as+形容词原级+as"（……的一半……）。例如：

My English is not half as good as yours. 我的英语不如你的一半好。

(3)"as...as"结构中，若形容词作定语修饰可数名词单数，不定冠词a（an）应置于形容词与名词之间。例如：

English is as important a subject as math. 英语是和数学同样重要的一门学科。

(4)"as...as"结构若指同一个人或物，则并无比较意义，而只是说明某人或某物具有两种性质，译为"又……又……"或"不但……而且……"。例如：

The boy is as strong as he is brave. 这个男孩又健壮又勇敢。

2. 形容词比较级的用法

(1) 表示两者之间比较时，用"形容词比较级+than"或"less...than"两种句型。例如：

Your mother looks healthier than before. 你妈妈看上去比以前健康了。

(2) 形容词的比较级还可以用于以下句型中。

①more and more...（越来越……）。例如：

The park is getting more and more beautiful. 这个公园变得越来越美了。

②the more...the...（越……就越……）。例如：

The more books we read, the cleverer we will become. 我们读的书越多，就会变得越聪明。

③the+比较级+of the two...（两个中较……的一个）。例如：

I'd like to go to the farther of the two places. 我愿意去两个地方中更远的那个地方。

④比较级+than any other+单数名词（比其他任何……都……）。例如：

The population of China is larger than any other's in the world. 中国的人口比世界上其他任何国家的人口都多。（暗指中国人口最多）

⑤形容词比较级前还可以用much, a lot, far, even, still, a little, no, any等表示程度的词来修饰。例如：

I feel a little better than yesterday. 我感觉比昨天好一点儿了。

3. 形容词最高级的用法

(1) 三者或三者以上相比较，用"the+最高级+名词+范围"结构。例如：

This is the cleanest place of the city. 这是这个城市最干净的地方。

Li Yun is the fastest of all the girls in our class. 李云是我们班女生中跑得最快的。

(2) 表示"最……之一"，用"one of the+形容词最高级+复数名词"。例如：

The Great Wall of China is one of the greatest buildings in the world. 中国的长城是世界上最伟大的建筑之一。

练 习

I. 选择题。

1. His son is going camping with _____ boys.
    A. little two other   B. two little other
    C. two other little   D. little other two

2. One day they crossed the _____ bridge behind the palace.
    A. old Chinese stone   B. Chinese old stone
    C. old stone Chinese   D. Chinese stone old

3. — How was your recent visit to Qingdao?
    — It was great. We visited some friends, and spent the _____ days at the seaside.
    A. few last sunny   B. last few sunny
    C. last sunny few   D. few sunny last

4. — Are you feeling _____?
    — Yes, I'm fine now.
    A. any well   B. any better   C. quite good   D. quite better

5. The experiment was _____ easier than we had expected.
    A. more   B. much more   C. much   D. more much

6. If there were no examinations, we should have _____ at school.
    A. the happiest time   B. a more happier time
    C. much happiest time   D. a much happier time

7. The weather in China is different from _____.
    A. in America   B. one in America
    C. America   D. that in America

8. After the new technique was introduced, the factory produced _____ tractors in 1988 as the year before.
    A. as twice many   B. as many twice
    C. twice as many   D. twice many as

9. John has three sisters, Mary is the _____ of the three.
    A. most cleverest   B. more clever
    C. cleverest   D. cleverer

10. She told us _____ story that we all forget about the time.
    A. such an interesting   B. such interesting a
    C. so an interesting   D. a so interesting

11. The story sounds _____.
    A. to be true   B. as true
    C. being true   D. true

Unit 5

12. The pianos in the other shop will be _____ , but _____ .
    A. cheaper, not as better   B. more cheap, not as better
    C. cheaper, not as good   D. more cheap, not as good
13. — How did you find your visit to the museum?
    — I thoroughly enjoyed it. It was _____ than I expected.
    A. far more interesting   B. even much interesting
    C. so more interesting   D. a lot much interesting
14. _____ food you've cooked!
    A. How a nice   B. What a nice
    C. How nice   D. What nice
15. These oranges taste _____ .
    A. good   B. well   C. to be good   D. to be well
16. John is _____ this year than last year.
    A. very taller   B. more taller
    C. much more taller   D. much taller
17. Canada is larger than _____ country in Asia.
    A. any   B. any other   C. other   D. another
18. Which is _____ country, Canada or Australia?
    A. a large   B. larger   C. a larger   D. the larger
19. — Mum, I think I'm _____ to get back to school.
    — Not really, my dear. You'd better to stay at home for another day or two.
    A. so well   B. so good   C. well enough   D. good enough
20. John was so sleepy that he could hardly keep his eyes _____ .
    A. open   B. to be opened C. to open   D. opening

Ⅱ. 用形容词的比较级填空。

1. He is 14 years old. His friend is 12 years old.
   His friend is _____ _____ he.
2. Our bikes are not the same as theirs.
   Our bikes are _____ _____ theirs.
3. He is healthier than his friend.
   He _____ _____ _____ of the two.
4. The girl is smarter than her classmates.
   The girl is smarter than _____ _____ in her class.
5. He is less popular than her.
   He is not _____ popular _____ her. She is _____ _____ than him.

93

Part Seven Writing

Request for Leave

Directions: In this part, you are going to learn how to write a *Request for Leave* and then try your hand.

1. Read the following sample.

Oct. 28, 2011

Dear Prof. Brown,

  I'm very sorry to tell you that I've got a bad cold. I'm feeling so terrible that I am unable to attend your lectures today. So, I'm writing to ask for a sick leave of one day. Enclosed is a medical certificate from the doctor. I should appreciate it if you grant me the leave.

Yours faithfully,
Zhang Hua

2. Translate the following passage into English.

尊敬的彼德森教授：

  非常抱歉，由于我正在发烧，身体感觉非常不舒服，所以今天不能去听您的课了，需要请假一天。随信附上医生开的病假条。如您能准假，我将不胜感激。

您诚挚的学生，
王敏
2011年10月30日

Data Bank

I have got a cold.	我感冒了。
I'm having a fever.	我正在发烧。
I have something wrong with my stomach.	我的胃出了毛病。
I haven't been feeling very well these days.	这几天我一直感觉不舒服。
I'm feeling terrible.	我觉得很难受。
I want to ask for a sick leave for one day.	我想请一天病假。
I enclose a medical certificate from the doctor.	随信附上医生开的病假条。
I should appreciate it if you grant me the leave.	如蒙准假我将十分感激。

Unit 5

Tips

写英语便条时必须将日期写明，并置于便条的右上角。年、月、日虽然可以全部用数字表示，但是，由于不同的英语国家对用数字表示的日期的理解不同，所以最好不要完全使用数字，以免造成不必要的误会。

Culture Notes

The Characteristics of English Names

An English full name consists of a person's first name and last name. First name is also called Christian name, given name or baptismal name. Last name is also called family name or surname. Sometimes, there is a middle name between the first name and the last name; middle name is also called second name.

The first name is a personal name given by his or her parents at some point after the birth of the child. It is also called a person's forename or personal name. The first name is informal, which is usually used among family members or close friends and colleagues.

The last name is a person's family name or surname, which is common to all members of the family. It is formal and often used on official occasions or with people you do not know well. The first name can be used as an informal form of address. But the family name is often used with a form of address before it, such as Mr. Brown, Mrs. Green, etc. Usually it cannot be used as a form of address alone.

Historically, a woman in England would assume her new husband's family name after marriage, and this remains common practice in the United Kingdom today as well as in other English-speaking countries. Traditionally, only women do so, but sometimes men as well change their last names upon marriage, assuming their wives' family names. Normally, a name change requires a legal procedure. Anyone who either marries or divorces may change his or her name if he or she wishes.

Unit 6

Money

 Part One Warm-up

1. Think of terms related to money and put them in the following box.

2. Do you agree with the old saying "Money makes the mare go"?
3. Do you think money can buy happiness?
4. Which would you prefer, wealth or health?

Unit 6

Part Two Speaking and Listening

Section A Listen to the following conversation and then repeat.

David: Hello, Sandy! Can you do me a favor?
Sandy: Hi, Tom. What is it?
David: I hate to say this, but can you lend me some cash? I lost my wallet.
Sandy: Sure. How much do you need?
David: Do you have 10 dollars? I have to buy a book.
Sandy: Uh, let me check. Yes. Here you are.
David: Thank you very much.
Sandy: You are welcome.

Section B Listen to the following short passage and fill in the missing words.

　　Spending 1) _____ is very important. As we are on the difficult times, you should keep in mind how much is your income and budget. Don't go spending beyond what you can 2) _____. Live within your 3) _____. Self discipline and common sense play a major part here. And only you, have the 4) _____ on your own spending habit. Be 5) _____ and wise when it comes to money spending.

Part Three Detailed Reading

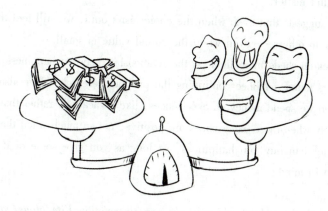

Can Money Really Buy Happiness

It turns out that whoever said money can't buy you happiness was wrong.

Money can buy you happiness, as long as you give some of the money away, or use it for an experience rather than buying a product.

In 2008, some researchers in the U.S. conducted three studies about the relationship between Americans' spending habits and their self-reported happiness. The first study was a national survey conducted on 632 Americans. The participants were asked to detail their income and spending habits. They were also asked to rate their general happiness level.

The researchers found that two things were significantly correlated with greater general happiness levels: higher income and spending on gifts for other people or giving money to charity. Although past research has been inconsistent in its finding that rich people are happier than people who are less well off, a recent research in 2009 finds that the wealthy are indeed considerably happier than those with average or poor incomes.

One could argue, "Of course, having more income can make you happy." But maybe it's related to either the dollar amount given, or the fact that people who are more likely to give money to others or to charity are just happier people by character. So the researchers set out to examine those suppositions in two separate follow-up experiments.

In a small, second study, 16 employees were asked about their general happiness levels before and after receiving their annual bonus. No matter what the size of the actual bonus, employees who spent more of their bonus money on others or charity reported greater general happiness levels than those who spent more of it on themselves.

Finally, in a third study of 46 people, researchers' discovery is very interesting. Those participants who were directed to spend a small amount of money on others (either $5 or $20) reported greater feelings of happiness than those who spent the same amounts on themselves. Again, the dollar amount didn't matter.

The third study suggests that even when the choice isn't ours, we still feel the happiness effects of giving away money to others — even when the actual value is small.

Other recent research sheds more light on the relationship between happiness and money, too. In 2009, some researchers found evidence confirming the previous research. They also proved that we are generally happier when we spend money on experiences, like a vacation, rather than on material things. But, we're happier only when those experiences are positive, not so much when they are negative.

So indeed, money can buy you happiness, as long as you give some of it away. Is it a good thing for you to keep in mind?

(This text is adapted from http://www.pbs.org/thisemotionallife/blogs/can-money-really-buy-happiness, 2011-12-13.)

Unit 6

New Words

conduct	[kən'dʌkt]	v.	to organize and direct (a particular activity) 实施
self-reported	['selfri'pɔːtid]	adj.	reported by oneself 自我报告的
survey	['sɜːvei]	n.	a set of questions that you ask a large number of people in order to find out about their opinions or behaviour 调查
	[sə'vei]	v.	to ask a large number of people questions in order to find out their attitudes or opinions 调查，审视
participant	[pɑː'tisipənt]	n.	someone who is taking part in an activity or event 参与者
detail	['diːteil]	v.	to list things or give all the facts or information about something 详述
		n.	a particular fact or item of information 细节，详情
rate	[reit]	v.	to estimate the value or quality of somebody or something 估价，定等级
correlated	['kɔrəˌleitid]	adj.	mutually related 相互关联的
charity	['tʃæriti]	n.	an organization that gives money, goods, or help to people who are poor, sick etc. 慈善，慈善机构
inconsistent	[ˌinkən'sistənt]	adj.	lack of consistency or agreement 不一致的
argue	['ɑːgjuː]	v.	to present reasons and arguments 争论，辩论，认为
supposition	[ˌsʌpə'ziʃən]	n.	a message expressing an opinion based on incomplete evidence 假设，推测，推想
bonus	['bəunəs]	n.	an extra amount of money given to someone as a reward for work or as encouragement 红利，奖金
employee	[ˌemplɔi'iː]	n.	a person who is paid to work for someone else 雇员
suggest	[sə'dʒest]	v.	to show (an idea or feeling) without stating it directly 暗示
			to mention (an idea, possible plan, or action) for other people to consider 提议，建议
evidence	['evidəns]	n.	basis for belief or disbelief; knowledge on which to base belief 根据，证据
confirm	[kən'fɜːm]	v.	to show that something is definitely true, especially by providing more proof 证实
previous	['priːvjəs]	adj.	happening or existing before the one mentioned 在……之前的，以前的

Phrases & Expressions

1. **turn out**: to happen in a particular way, or to have a particular result, especially one that you did not expect 结果是……

   例: Even the best theory can turn out to be wrong. 即便是最好的理论, 也有可能被证明是错误的。

2. **give away**: make a gift of 送掉, 分发

   例: He wants to give away all his modern possessions and return to nature. 他要舍弃一切时髦的东西而返璞归真。

3. **correlate with**: to be closely connected to each other 使……与……发生关系, 把……与……联系起来

   例: Results in the natural sciences seldom seem to correlate with those in art. 自然科学的成果似乎很少与艺术发生关联。

4. **well off**: having a lot of money, or enough money to have a good standard of living 富有的

   例: If he had worked harder when young, he would be well off now. 如果他年轻时多努力一点, 现在就能过得舒服些。

5. **set out**: to leave a place and begin a journey; to start doing something or making plans to do something in order to achieve a particular result 出发; 开始

   例: They set out on the last stage of their journey. 他们开始了旅行的最后一程。

6. **shed light on**: to make something easier to understand, by providing new or better information 阐明, 把……弄清楚

   例: These discoveries may shed light on the origins of the universe. 这些发现会有助于理解宇宙的起源。

Comprehension of the Text

Choose the best answer for each of the following questions.

1. According to the author, when can money buy people happiness? _____
   A. When people spend money on themselves.
   B. When people spend money on products.
   C. When people give some of the money away.
   D. When people have a lot of money.

2. What are the things that are closely related to greater general happiness levels? _____
   A. Higher income
   B. Spending on gifts for other people
   C. Money given to charity
   D. All of the above

3. According to the research, which of the following is TRUE? _____
   A. People who spent more money on themselves are happier than those who spent more money on others or charity.
   B. People who spent money voluntarily on others are happier than those who were directed to spend money on others.
   C. People who spent more money are happier than those who spent less money.
   D. People who spent more money on others or charity are happier than those who spent more on themselves.
4. What is the information that other recent research provides? _____
   A. The previous research is wrong.
   B. People are also generally happier when they spend money on buying something.
   C. People are also generally happier when they spend money on their experiences.
   D. People feel the same happiness when they spend money on experiences and on products.
5. What can we infer from the text? _____
   A. Giving is better than receiving.
   B. Money makes the mare go.
   C. Wealth is better than poverty.
   D. Money is the root of all evils.

Part Four   Exercises

Task 1   Choose the definition from Column B that best matches each word or phrase in Column A.

A	B
1. inconsistent	a. an organization that gives money, goods, or help to people who are poor, sick etc.
2. survey	b. an extra amount of money given to someone as a reward for work or as encouragement
3. participant	c. a person who is paid to work for someone else
4. charity	d. a set of questions that you ask a large number of people in order to find out about their opinions or behaviors
5. annual	e. having a lot of money, or enough money to have a good standard of living
6. bonus	f. a holiday, or time spent not on working
7. employee	g. of or for a period of one year
8. well off	h. someone who is taking part in an activity or event

9. vacation
10. negative

i. expressing or meaning a refusal or denial
j. lack of consistency or agreement

Task 2 Fill in the blanks with the words or expressions given below. Change the form where necessary.

| suggest | confirm | positive | correlate with | shed light on |
| turn out | previous | give away | set out | conduct |

1. Before the invention of the mouse, people _____ on the screen of a computer by a special pen.
2. A good teacher should have the ability to _____ the abstract and complex problems so that students can easily understand them.
3. The result of this experiment does not _____ the result of earlier one.
4. He decided to _____ everything he possessed and become a monk (和尚).
5. She's applied for a lot of jobs recently, which _____ that she's not altogether happy with her position.
6. Darwin _____ to question views about how life had developed on the earth.
7. Health officials _____ that there's a flu epidemic underway.
8. Do you have any _____ experience of this type of work?
9. As it _____ he passed the exam quite easily.
10. We need to take _____ steps to improve the situation of families in poverty.

Task 3 Translate the following sentences into English, paying special attention to the underlined parts.

1. 原来他们还是孩子的时候，她就认识他了。（it turned out that）
2. 真的有必要在动物身上进行实验吗？（conduct）
3. 他的研究成果和你的研究成果有关联。（correlate with）
4. 什么是最有可能发生的？（be likely to）
5. 最近的研究有助于弄清疾病的起因。（shed light on）

Part Five Supplementary Reading

How to Make the Most of Your Money in School

Trying to learn how to manage and save your money while in school can be a challenge. With these guidelines, however, you can set yourself down the path toward financial responsibility.

Make a Budget before You Arrive

Figure out what your "income" is (payments from student loans, campus job paychecks, and/or help from Mom and Dad). Then figure out what your "expenses" are, and when they're due. Once you have those figures for the semester or the year, break them down into what your income and expenses will be each month. As long as your income is more than your expenses, you're in great shape and can make a budget.

Get a Campus Job

If, after making your budget, you find that you would like, or even need, some additional income, consider finding an on-campus job. Most students work while attending school. On-campus jobs are often much friendlier to student needs than off-campus jobs.

Use Your Student Discount

No matter where you're going to school, the nearby and surrounding communities are used to having students around. Often, restaurants, bookstores, movie theaters, travel agencies, clothing shops, and all kinds of other stores will offer discounts to local students. Don't be afraid to ask if places will offer you a student discount if you show your student ID. You may be pleasantly surprised by where you can save money!

Think Creatively

You're in college because you're smart. So use your head! Can you save money by buying used books instead of new ones? Can you buy a few items at the grocery store, such as cereal and milk, that you can keep in your room to avoid having to pay higher prices in the campus dining hall? Can you adjust your meal plan to a less-expensive option? Spend a day taking notes in a notebook about all the places where you spend money, and what you spend it on. Then use that big brain of yours to think creatively about other options.

Try to Avoid Using Credit Cards

Credit cards can be a lifesaver to a lot of people, but they come at a high cost. Credit card debt can rack up quickly, and increasing numbers of college students are getting into financial trouble by using their credit cards during their college years. Only use a credit card if absolutely necessary.

Most students head to college looking forward to becoming independent and managing their lives on their own. Managing your money is part of that independence. Starting early, and starting strong, will help ensure that your college experience is spent focusing on the fun stuff instead of the financial part! Remember: if you're good to your money, it will be good to you.

(This text is adapted from http://collegelife.about.com/od/moneyfinances/a/Managing_Money.htm, 2011-12-09.)

New Words

challenge	['tʃælindʒ]	n.	something that tests strength, skill, or ability, especially in a way that is interesting 挑战
guideline	['gaidlain]	n.	rules or instructions about the best way to do something 指引，指导方针
budget	['bʌdʒit]	n.	the money that is available to an organization or person, or a plan of how it will be spent 预算
additional	[ə'diʃənl]	adj.	more than what was agreed or expected 附加的，另外的
discount	['diskaunt]	n.	a reduction in the usual price of something 折扣
ID	['ai'di:]	n.	a document that shows one's name and date of birth, usually with a photograph (=identification) 身份证
grocery (store)	['grəusəri]	n.	a store where food and small items for the house are sold 食品杂货店
cereal	['siəriəl]	n.	a plant grown to produce grain, for example, wheat, rice etc. 谷类食物
adjust	[ə'dʒʌst]	v.	to gradually become familiar with a new situation 调整，适应

| option | [ˈɒpʃən] | n. | a choice you can make in a particular situation 选择（权），可选物 |

credit card   a small plastic card that you use to buy goods or services and pay for them later 信用卡

| ensure | [inˈʃuə] | v. | to make certain that an event or activity will happen properly 保证，确保 |

Phrases & Expressions

1. figure out: to understand somebody or something, or to find the answer (to something) by thinking 想出，解决
   例：It took her a long time to figure out who the wrongdoer was. 她用了很长时间才琢磨出谁是做坏事的人。

2. break down: to divide (something) into smaller parts 分解
   例：After many years, rocks break down into dirt. 许多年以后，岩石分解成为泥土。

3. in shape: in a good state of health or physical fitness 处于良好状态
   例：Mary was putting her French in shape for the test. 玛丽已为法语考试做好了充分的准备。

4. rack up: to get a number or amount of something 积累
   例：The team has racked up ten points to win the game. 这个队已经得了十分，要赢这场比赛了。

5. look forward to: to feel pleasure because an event or activity is going to happen 盼望，期待
   例：We look forward to the return of spring. 我们期待着春天的到来。

6. focus on: to give special attention to one particular person or thing, or to make people do this 集中（注意力、精力等）于……
   例：They must focus on the quality of the products. 他们必须注重产品的质量。

Comprehension Questions

Answer the following questions according to the text.

1. What is the text mainly about?
2. What are the five ways of making the most of your money? Which do you think is most useful for you?
3. What are your ways of making the best of your money while at college?

Part Six Grammar

副词（Adverbs）

副词主要用来修饰动词、形容词或其他结构。副词分为如下八种：

（1）方式副词。如 bravely（勇敢地），fast（快），happily（愉快地），hard（艰难地），quickly（快），well（好）。

（2）地点副词。如 by（近旁），down（下），here（这里），near（附近），there（那里），up（上）。

（3）时间副词。如 now（现在），soon（不久），still（仍然），then（那时），today（今天），yet（迄今）。

（4）频度副词。如 always（总是），never（从不），occasionally（偶尔），often（时常），twice（两次）。

（5）句子副词。如 certainly（当然），definitely（一定），luckily（幸运地），surely（确实）。

（6）程度副词。如 fairly（相当），hardly（几乎不），rather（十分），quite（非常），too（也），very（很）。

（7）疑问副词。如 when（何时），where（何地），why（为何）。

（8）关系副词。如 when（何时），where（何地），why（为何）。

一、副词的形式

1. 一般形式：形容词+ly

许多方式副词和一些程度副词是由相应的形容词加 ly 构成的。如：immediate—immediately；slow—slowly。

形容词加 ly 变副词时要注意下列变化规则：

（1）词尾的 y 变为 i，如 happy—happily。

（2）词尾的 e 保留不变，如 extreme—extremely。但也有例外情况，如：true—truly；due—duly；whole—wholly。

（3）以 able/ible 结尾的形容词去掉词尾的 e 再加 y，如：capable—capably；sensible—sensibly。

（4）以"元音+l"结尾的形容词按常例加 ly，如：beautiful—beautifully；final—finally。

2. 特殊情况

good 的副词形式是 well。

kindly 可作形容词也可作副词。除此以外，以 ly 结尾的形容词，如 friendly，likely，lonely 等，没有副词形式，表示其副词意义时通常使用一个与其意义相似的副词或副词短语。例如：

likely（形容词）—probably（副词）

friendly（形容词）—in a friendly way（副词短语）

二、副词含义的变化

一些副词与它们相应的形容词相比含义较窄，如 coldly（冷酷地），coolly（冷淡），hotly（热情地），warmly（亲热地），这些词主要用于表达感情方面。

还有些副词与其相应的形容词意思不同。例如：

They treated us coldly. 他们对我们很冷淡。（不友好地）

She welcomed us warmly. 她向我们表示热烈欢迎。（友好地）

但是，warmly dressed 相当于 wearing clothes（穿着很暖和的衣服）。

另外，coolly 相当于 calmly（冷静地）、courageously（勇敢地）或 impudently（无礼或不敬地）。例如：

He behaved very coolly when they are in danger. 在这个危险的处境中他表现得镇定自若。

presently 相当于 soon（不久）。例如：

He'll be here presently. 他马上就到这里。

三、副词的位置

副词的位置主要有下列几种：

（1）在动词之前；

（2）在 be 动词、助动词之后；

（3）有多个助动词时，副词一般放在第一个助动词后。

有下列两点需要注意：

（1）大多数方式副词位于句尾，但宾语过长时，副词可以提前，以使句子平衡。例如：

We could see very clearly that he is lying. 我们很清楚地看到他在撒谎。

（2）方式副词 well，badly，hard 等只放在句尾。例如：

He speaks English well. 他的英语说得很好。

四、副词的排列顺序

（1）时间、地点副词，小单位在前，大单位在后。例如：

in shanghai, China 在中国，上海　　in the afternoon of wednesday 在星期三下午

（2）方式副词，短的在前，长的在后，并用 and 或 but 等连词连接。例如：

Please write slowly and carefully. 请慢慢地、小心地写。

（3）多个不同副词的排列顺序：程度+地点+方式+时间副词。例如：

The children played games quietly in their room yesterday. 这些孩子昨天在教室里静静地玩游戏。

有下列两点需要注意：

（1）副词 very 可以修饰形容词，但不能修饰动词。例如：

（错）I very like her.

（对）I like her very much.

（2）副词 enough 要放在形容词的后面，形容词 enough 放在名词的前后均可。例如：

I don't know him well enough. 我不太了解他。

There is enough food for everyone to eat.

There is food enough for everyone to eat. 食物足够大家吃。

五、副词的比较级和最高级的变化规则

1. 规则变化

双音节或多音节副词构成比较级时，要在其前加 more，构成最高级时则加 most。例如：

carefully—more carefully—most carefully

单音节副词以及副词 early 则在词尾加 er 与 est。例如：

hard—harder—hardest

early—earlier—earliest（注意变 y 为 i）

2. 不规则变化

一些副词的比较级和最高级的不规则变化如下：

well—better—best

badly—worse—worst

little—less—least

much—more—most

far—farther—farthest（仅用于指距离）

(far—further—furthest)

六、某些副词之后的倒装

某些副词和副词短语，主要是一些含有限定或否定意义的副词和副词短语，为了表示强调，可放在句首，这时后面应跟动词的倒装（即疑问）形式。这类副词或副词短语中最重要的有：hardly ever, on no account, hardly...when, only by, under no circumstances, only in this way, neither/nor, only then/when, never, scarcely ever, no sooner...than, scarcely...when, not only, seldom, not till, so, nowhere。例如：

Hardly had I entered the room when the telephone rang. 我一进家门，电话铃就响了。

Seldom did he visit his parents. 他很少去看望父母。

So interesting was the book that he did not put it down till he finished it. 这本书太有意思了，他拿起就一直舍不得放下，直到读完为止。

七、一些副词的区别与用法

1. fairly, rather

（1）这两个词都有"相当""适中"的意思，但 fairly 主要用于修饰褒义的形容词和副词（如 bravely, good, nice, well 等），而 rather 主要修饰贬义的形容词和副词（如 bad, stupidly, ugly 等）。例如：

John is fairly clever, but Peter is rather stupid. 约翰相当聪明，而彼得就颇笨。

（2）rather 可用在 alike, like, similar, different 等词及比较级之前，这时它的含义是"少许"或"略微"。例如：

The result was rather worse than I had expected. 结果比我预料的还坏。

另外，rather a 可以与一些名词连用，如 disappointment, disadvantage, nuisance, pity, shame 及 joke。例如：

It's rather a nuisance that we can't park here. 真讨厌，我们不能在这里停车。（有点儿不方便）

It's rather a shame that she has to work on Sundays. 真讨厌，她连星期天也得去上班。（有点儿不公平）

fairly 则不能这样用。

（3）rather 可以用在某些褒义的形容词和副词之前，如 amusing, clever, good, pretty, well 等，此时它几乎相当于 very 之意，没有贬义，例如：

She is rather clever. 她很聪明。

（4）rather 也可用在 enjoy 与 like 这两个词前，有时还可用在 dislike 与 object 这一类动词之前。例如：

I rather like the smell of petrol. 我倒很喜欢汽油味儿。

2. quite

（1）quite 与一些表示"完整""完全"意思的词或词组（如 all right, certain, determined, empty, finish, ready, right, sure, wrong 等），或与一些具有强烈感情色彩的形容词、副词（如 amazing, extraordinary, horrible, perfect 等）连用时，它的意思是"完全地""全然地"。例如：

You're quite wrong. 你完全错了。

It's quite strange; I can't understand it at all. 这件事太奇怪了，我根本没法理解。

（2）在与其他形容词、副词连用时，quite 略有减弱这些形容词或副词的程度的作用，因此 quite good 赞誉的程度要比 good 轻。quite 这样用时，其含义类似 fairly，但它的强度根据它被重读的方式可以有很大的不同，具体如下：

quite′good（quite 弱读，good 强读）表示只比 good 稍稍弱一点。

′quite′good（两个词重读的强弱程度相同）意思是"还算好"。

′quite good（quite 强读，good 弱读）表示远不如 good。

也就是说，quite 的读音越轻，紧跟在它后面的形容词或副词的意思就越重。

此外，还要注意冠词 a/an 与 quite 连用时的位置。例如：

quite a long walk 一次较长的散步

quite an old castle 一座较古老的城堡

3. hardly, scarcely, barely

这三个词在意义上都接近于否定。

（1）hardly 主要与 any, ever, at all 或动词 can 连用。例如：

He has hardly any money. 他几乎没有钱。（非常少）

I hardly ever go out. 我很少外出。（极少外出）

（2）scarcely 意为"几乎不"，它可以代替 hardly。比如，上述例句中也可用 scarcely any/scarcely ever 等。但 scarcely 主要意为"不到""不足"。例如：

There were scarcely thirty people there. 那儿连 30 个人都没有。

（3）barely 意为"不超过""仅仅"。例如：

There were barely thirty people there. 那儿不超过 30 个人。（刚刚 30 个）

I can barely see it. 我勉强看得见它。（只能看见而已）

练习

选择题。

1. The twenty-year-old young man is _____ carry that heavy bag.
   A. strong enough to   B. enough strong to
   C. not strong enough   D. strong enough

2. Yang won the women's 500 meters in the sports meeting. She did _____ of all.
   A. best   B. better   C. well   D. good

3. — It's so cold today.
   — Yes, it's _____ colder than it was yesterday.
   A. some   B. more   C. very   D. much

4. — _____ did it _____ the conductor to check the tickets this morning?
   — Half an hour.
   A. How soon; take   B. How long; cost
   C. How often; spent   D. How long; take

5. — Excuse me, _____ is the nearest bookshop?
   — Go down the street and turn left at the second corner.
   A. how   B. what   C. where   D. who

6. — _____ is it from our school to Lupu Bridge?
   — About half an hour's bus ride. Shall we go and visit it?
   A. How long   B. How often   C. How far   D. How much

7. Tom does his homework _____ Lucy.
   A. as carefully as   B. so careful as
   C. as careful as   D. so carefully as

8. Pass my glasses to me, Jack. I can _____ read the words in the newspapers.
   A. hardly   B. really   C. rather   D. clearly

9. — Please write to me when you have time.
   — Sure. But _____ is your e-mail address?
   A. when   B. where   C. what   D. which

10. — How far is it from your home to your school?
    — It's a quarter's walk, _____.
    A. here and there   B. now and then
    C. up and down   D. more or less

11. — It's a nice car. _____ have you been in it?
    — Just to Shanghai.
    A. How much   B. How long   C. How soon   D. How far

12. — _____ were you away from school last year?

— About two weeks.

    A. How often   B. How soon   C. How long   D. When

13. — George looks strong. Has he ever been sick?

    — He's a superman! He _____ goes to the doctor.

    A. already   B. even   C. often   D. seldom

14. — Does Liu Hua ever guess the meanings of English words?

    — He _____ guesses the meanings of new words. He uses his dictionary all the time.

    A. usually   B. always   C. never   D. sometimes

15. You must drive _____ next time, or there may be another accident.

    A. more carefully   B. carefully

    C. careful   D. more careful

16. — _____ do you go to the library?

    — Four times a month.

    A. How often   B. How soon   C. How long   D. How much

17. I can't say _____ I want to see you again. It's a year since I last saw you.

    A. how long   B. how often   C. how much   D. how soon

18. Don't worry, sir. I'm sure I can run _____ to catch up with them.

    A. slowly enough   B. enough slowly

    C. fast enough   D. enough fast

19. This question is _____ more difficult than that one.

    A. rather   B. quite   C. very   D. a little

20. There was _____ to weight the elephant.

    A. nothing enough big   B. big nothing enough

    C. nothing big enough   D. big enough nothing

 Part Seven   Writing

Posters

Directions: In this part, you are going to learn how to write a *Poster* and then try your hand.

1. Read the following sample.

> Exciting Basketball Match
> Chinese Dept. VS. English Dept.
> Time: 3:00 p.m. Wednesday, March 29
> Place: the Campus Stadium

2. Translate the following poster into English.

> **IT 业专题讲座**
>
> 内容：IT 产业的发展趋势
> 报告人：约翰森教授
> 主办：计算机科学系
> 时间：3 月 20 日（星期二）下午 3 点
> 地点：教学楼 A 座小报告厅

Data Bank

match	（球类）比赛
race	（速度类）比赛
competition	（技巧类）比赛
tournament	锦标赛，联赛
championship	锦标赛，冠军赛
vs. = versus	（比赛用语）……对……
contest	竞赛
performance	表演
concert	音乐会
exhibition	展览
show	表演，放电影
lecture	讲座
seminar	研讨会

Tips

海报（Poster）多以醒目的方式来宣传或通告即将发生的活动，如晚会、讲座、报告会以及体育比赛等。海报简单明了，常附有插图，内容包含活动的时间、地点、内容等。如有必要，还要将主办方和参与人员介绍清楚。

Unit 7

Internet

Part One   Warm-up

1. Think of terms related to Internet and put them in the following box.

2. Do you usually get access to the Internet?
3. What do you often do on the Internet?
4. How does the Internet influence your life?

Part Two Speaking and Listening

Section A Listen to the following conversation and then repeat.

David: Do you know much about the Internet?
Sandy: Not a great deal.
David: I've just been reading an article about them. It can be used to do many things now.
Sandy: For reading news, sending emails and chatting with friends?
David: Yes, but they're used for other things too. Do you remember how we bought our tickets for the flight to France?
Sandy: Sure.
David: I booked the tickets online. A few hours later somebody sent us our tickets.
Sandy: Of course. That is online shopping.
David: That is right.

Section B Listen to the following short passage and fill in the missing words.

EBay is one of the most popular 1) _____ for shopping online. Consumers have a 2) _____ of reasons for preferring online shopping to shopping at retail 3) _____. One of the main reasons for shopping online is 4) _____. Another reason to shop online is better prices. When you shop online you get the chance to 5) _____ prices from several different online retailers. People also prefer online shopping because it allows them to research products without receiving biased pressure from sales associates.

Part Three Detailed Reading

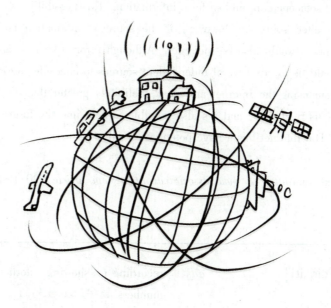

How the Internet has Influenced Our Lives

We all agree that the Internet, along with other digital media, plays a big role in our lives. But do we ever realize how the Internet can change us? The rapidly growing web of information, the Internet, has many positive results for our society. The Internet will play an increasingly large role in our lives in the future.

The Internet has a huge potential to advance our society. With such a big web of information and such a vast group of tools, it allows ordinary people to do things that only specialists could do 10 years ago, and gives scientists and researchers the ability to test things once unimaginable.

The Internet is known to be a great communication tool. Social networking sites like Facebook and MySpace allow people to connect with others and correspond with friends. Instant messaging software like Windows Live Messenger let people hold live conversations without having to meet each other. E-mailing is an alternate way of communicating with others. Communication is one of the most important capabilities of the Internet.

Many people also use the Internet for news. On news websites, people can check the weather, traffic, and anything else they need. People can also use the Internet to find out information they need, like bus schedules and store hours, just to name a few.

Another very important use for the Internet is shopping. Many people buy things from

Amazon.com, for the reason that buying things online and having them shipped straight to your house is a lot more convenient than going to a store and buying them. Similar to shopping online, downloading software has become very popular. There is a lot of free software that people can use.

We know that the Internet is very powerful, and plenty of information can be found on it. However, what happens when the information is false? With sites like Wikipedia, where anyone can edit the information, someone can publish false information. This possibility is countered by the fact that articles require cited sources. However, if the source's information is incorrect, then the information on Wikipedia would also be incorrect. Although errors like this can happen, a simple way to prevent it would be to cite several independent sources to check for errors.

The benefits from using the Internet are great, definitely greater than the disadvantages. We can see that it helps us right now, and it's also possible to look into the future and see how it can benefit us later on. The Internet has a huge potential for all of us.

(This text is adapted from http://www.associatedcontent.com/article, 2011-12-03.)

New Words

digital	[ˈdidʒitl]	adj.	recording or showing information in the form of numbers 数字的，数码的
information	[ˌinfəˈmeiʃən]	n.	facts or details that tell you something about a situation, person, event etc. 信息，情报，新闻，资料
potential	[pəˈtenʃl]	adj.	likely to develop into a particular type of person or thing in the future 可能的，潜在的
		n.	the possibility that something will develop in a particular way, or have a particular effect 潜力，潜能
advance	[ədˈvɑːns]	v.	to go or move (something) forward, or to develop or improve (something) 前进，增长
specialist	[ˈspeʃəlist]	n.	someone who knows a lot about a particular subject, or is very skilled at it 专家
network	[ˈnetwəːk]	n.	a group formed from parts that are connected together 网络，系统
correspond	[ˌkɔrisˈpɔnd]	v.	to exchange messages or letters 通信，联络
instant	[ˈinstənt]	adj.	happening immediately 立即的，即时的
		n.	a very short moment of time, or a particular point in time 立即，瞬间
live	[laiv]	adj.	actually being performed at the time of hearing or

			viewing 直播的
alternate	[ɔːlˈtɜːnit]	adj.	(of sets of two) every second, or every other 交替的，轮流的，间隔的
	[ˈɔːltəneit]	v.	to cause (two things) to happen or exist one after the other repeatedly 交替，轮流
communication	[kəˌmjuːniˈkeiʃən]	n.	the process by which people exchange information or express their thoughts and feelings 沟通，交通，信息
capability	[ˌkeipəˈbiləti]	n.	the natural ability, skill, or power 能力，才能，性能
traffic	[ˈtræfik]	n.	pedestrians or vehicles coming and going 交通
schedule	[ˈskedʒul]	n.	a list of planned activities or things to be done at or during a particular time 时间表，一览表，计划
		vt.	to plan something for a particular time 安排，计划
ship	[ʃip]	v.	to transport by ship（用船）运送，装运，上（船）
convenient	[kənˈviːnjənt]	adj.	suited to your comfort, purpose or needs 方便的
download	[ˈdaunləud]	vt.	to move information or programs from a computer network to a small computer 下载
edit	[ˈedit]	v.	to prepare a book, piece of film etc. for printing or broadcasting by removing mistakes or parts that are not acceptable 编辑，编校，修订
publish	[ˈpʌbliʃ]	v.	to make available to the public, usually by printing a book, magazine, newspaper, or other document 出版，发行
counter	[ˈkauntə]	v.	to react (to something) with an opposing opinion or action 反对，反击
cite	[sait]	vt.	to mention something as an example, especially one that supports, proves, or explains an idea or situation 引用，引证
independent	[ˌindiˈpendənt]	adj.	not influenced or controlled by other people and free to make your own decisions 独立的，自主的
source	[sɔːs]	n.	something or somebody that causes or produces something, or is the origin of it 来源
benefit	[ˈbenifit]	n.	a helpful or good effect 利益
		v.	to be useful or profitable to 有益于；得益
disadvantage	[ˌdisədˈvɑːntidʒ]	n.	something that causes problems, or that makes

someone or something less likely to be successful or effective 不利，不利条件

Phrases & Expressions

1. **play a role**: to have an effect or influence on something 起作用；扮演角色
   例：Teachers should play a role of guide and service for students. 教师应该起到指导和服务于学生的作用。
2. **correspond with**: to write letters to someone and receive letters from them 和……通信
   例：I have corresponded with him for some years, but I have never met him in the flesh. 我和他通信联系已经好几年了，但一直未与他本人见过面。

Comprehension of the Text

Choose the best answer for each of the following questions.

1. The text mainly tells us that _____.
    A. the Internet has many negative influences on people's lives so it should be banned
    B. the Internet, having both positive and negative influence, plays an important role in our lives
    C. the Internet has so many advantages that we may use it without any worries
    D. although the Internet has big influence on our lives, it can not change us at all
2. Why does the Internet have huge potential to advance the society? _____
    A. Because it has a huge web of information.
    B. Because it has a vast group of tools.
    C. Because it is a great communication tool.
    D. Because it can help ordinary people and researchers and scientists do things which can not be done or imagined before.
3. What is the correct way to prevent the false information on the Internet? _____
    A. Don't allow people to edit the information on the Internet.
    B. Forbid people from publishing false information on the Internet.
    C. To cite several independent sources to check for errors.
    D. Ask the author to provide cited sources for the information.
4. According to the text, which of the following is NOT true? _____
    A. The Internet is a great communication tool.
    B. A large number of people dislike the Internet because it has some false information.
    C. A lot of people use the Internet for shopping.
    D. Many people use the Internet for news.
5. What's the author's attitude toward the Internet? _____

A. positive B. negative C. neutral D. indifference

 Part Four Exercises

Task 1 Choose the definition from Column B that best matches each word in Column A.

A	B
1. media	a. a group formed from parts that are connected together
2. information	b. the process by which people exchange information or express their thoughts and feelings
3. advance	c. the natural ability, skill, or power
4. communication	d. facts or details that tell you something about a situation, person, event etc.
5. instant	e. to react (to something) with an opposing opinion or action
6. capability	f. to go or move (something) forward, or to develop or improve (something)
7. counter	g. happening immediately
8. source	h. not influenced or controlled by other people but free to make your own decisions
9. independent	i. something or someone that causes or produces something, or is the origin of it
10. network	j. newspapers, magazines, television, and radio, considered as a group

Task 2 Fill in the blanks with the words or expressions given below. Change the form where necessary.

| digital | play a role | correspond with | potential | alternate |
| publish | cite | advantage | download | convenient |

1. The Internet is a very _____ way to communicate and share information with people all over the world.
2. We plan to begin _____ a newsletter on the Internet next month.
3. Computers use the binary (二进制) number system. A binary _____ is called a bit.
4. The screen can also display photos, text and _____ information from website.
5. He soon realized that he was in the team to _____ in the system.
6. Her rich experience gave her a(n) _____ over other applicants for the job.

7. I have been _____ my foreign friends for years.
8. The lawyer _____ a previous case to support his argument.
9. As a student, my life _____ between work and sleep.
10. Education can develop one's _____ abilities.

> Task 3 Translate the following sentences into English, paying special attention to the underlined parts.

1. 你一直在和你的中学同学通信吗？(correspond with)
2. 因特网在我们的学习和生活中扮演着重要的角色。(play a role)
3. 误会是由缺乏交流引起的。(communication)
4. 网上购物越来越受到人们，特别是年轻人的欢迎。(popular)
5. 总的来说，网络利大于弊。(advantage, disadvantage)

Part Five   Supplementary Reading

How to Overcome Internet Addiction

Internet addiction is something that's either laughed at or it's a serious problem. While not having the health effects of other types of dependencies, it can still be a problem if it gets in the way of work or social life. Don't be like a fly caught in the Web.

Instructions

Step 1: Recognize the problem. Do you check email often when it is not entirely necessary? Do you go back to the same websites again and again? How many hours a day do you spend surfing the web?

Step 2: Recognize the reasons. The Internet is always available and cheaper than alcohol addiction, and legal unlike drug addiction. It offers escape just like drugs and alcohol. Once you realize these reasons, you can discover Internet addiction as a real problem and not something to be laughed at as not being a "real" addiction.

Step 3: Cut down on Internet use. This is, of course, easier said than done. You can't stop checking email any more than you can stop checking the mail box. You can, however, stop checking it with the same frequency. Set the maximum amount you use the computer a day. This applies to chat rooms, games, online gambling, social networking sites, and other sites that take up your time.

Step 4: Take walks, go out to eat, leave your office or home — i.e. get away from the computer. Breaking away for a few hours can help clear the head. If you have wifi, don't take the computer with you.

Step 5: Start a new hobby, read a book, play games with a friend, play sports — try to find offline activities that fill up your time.

Tips & Warnings

As with any addiction, it is heartening to know that there are other people who suffer from the same problem. There are now support groups for this new and growing problem.

Call people up on the phone who you normally correspond with via email. Set up a face-to-face meeting.

As with any addiction, you must determine what you are trying to escape from. The addiction is the symptom, but you need to deal with the cause.

If none of the above works, seek professional counseling. Internet addiction can be as bad as other types of addiction if left unchecked.

(This text is adapted from http://www.ehow.com, 2011-12-05.)

New Words

dependency	[diˈpendənsi]	n.	a state of needing something or someone, especially in order to continue existing or operating 依赖，从属
surf	[sə:f]	v.	to move quickly from one place to another on the Internet to learn what each place is offering 网上冲浪，浏览
alcohol	[ˈælkəhɔl]	n.	drinks such as beer or wine that contain a substance which can make you drunk 酒，酒精
frequency	[ˈfri:kwənsi]	n.	the number of times that something happens within a particular period of time or within a particular group of people 频繁
maximum	[ˈmæksiməm]	adj.	being the largest amount or number allowed or possible 最高的，最大极限的

gambling	[ˈgæmbliŋ]	n.	activities in which people risk money or possessions on the result of something which is not certain, such as a card game or a horse race 赌博，投机
wifi	[ˈwaifai]	abbr.	(= Wireless Fidelity) n. [U] a system for connecting electronic equipment such as computers and electronic organizers to the Internet without using wires 无线局域网
heartening	[ˈhɑːtniŋ]	adj.	making you feel happier and more positive 振奋人心的
suffer	[ˈsʌfə]	v.	to experience or show the effects of something bad 遭受，忍受
symptom	[ˈsimptəm]	n.	any single problem which is caused by and shows a more serious and general problem 症状
professional	[prəˈfeʃənəl]	adj.	relating to a job that needs special education and training 专业的
counseling	[ˈkaunsəliŋ]	n.	the job or process of listening to someone and giving them advice about their problems 咨询服务

Phrases & Expressions

1. **get in the way**: block a road, someone's path etc. so that they cannot move forward easily 阻碍，妨碍

   例：No doubt he means to help, but in fact he just gets in the way. 他确实是想帮忙，然而事实上却只是帮倒忙。

2. **apply to**: to use something such as a method, idea, or law in a particular situation, activity, or process 适用于，运用于

   例：The laws apply to everyone irrespective of race, color, or creed. 法律对人人都适用，不分种族、肤色或信仰。

3. **take up**: to fill a particular amount of time or space 占去，占据

   例：I won't take up much of your time. 我不想多占用你的时间。

4. **break away**: to become loose and no longer attached to something 离开，逃脱

   例：You must break away from such bad habits. 你必须改掉这样的坏习惯。

5. **fill up**: to become full, or to make something become full 装满；填补

   例：This article will fill up a column of the paper. 这篇文章将排满报纸的一栏。

Comehension Questions

Answer the following questions according to the text.

1. When will Internet addiction be a problem?
2. How to reduce Internet use according to the author's instructions?
3. According to the author, what should you do if all the tips mentioned do not work?

 Part Six　Grammar

介词（Prepositions）

　　介词又叫前置词，通常位于名词或代词之前。介词是虚词，一般无句子重音，也不能单独做句子成分，必须与名词、代词或动名词构成介词短语在句中充当一个成分，表示人、物、事件等与其他人、物、事件等之间的关系。
　　介词可分为 3 类，具体如下：
　　（1）简单介词。如 at, in, on, by, to, of, for, off, about, with, over, near, past, down, along, till (until), like, before, after, above, below, since, behind, during, among, between, under, except, across, through, toward(s), against 等。
　　（2）合成介词。如 into, onto, inside, outside, without 等。
　　（3）短语介词。如 next to, instead of, in front of, from…to…, in the front of, at the back of, at the end of, by the end of, at the head of, in the middle of, because of, thanks to, out of 等。

一、介词的作用
介词在句子中充当的成分有以下 4 种。
（1）作定语。例如：
The man in the room is his brother. 房间里的这个人是他的哥哥。
（2）作状语。例如：
We get up at six.（表时间）我们 6 点起床。
They cancelled the sports meet because of the heavy rain.（表原因）由于大雨，他们取消了运动会。
We keep in touch by exchanging emails.（表方法）我们通过电子邮件保持联系。
（3）作表语。例如：
My dictionary is on the bookshelf. 我的字典在书架上。
（4）作宾语补足语。例如：
I found him in the office. 我在办公室找到了他。

二、介词的位置

介词通常位于名词或代词之前。然而，以下两个结构中的介词在非正式英语中有可能会移到句末。

（1）以介词+whom/which/what/whose/where 开头的疑问句。例如：

To whom did you give the present?（正式的）

Who did you give the present to?（非正式的）你把礼物送给谁了？

In which member does he have trust?（正式的）

Which member does he have trust in?（非正式的）他信任哪一个成员？

过去常常认为以介词结尾的句子是不合乎语法要求的，但是现在它已被接受为一种口语形式。

（2）在短语动词中，介词或副词跟在动词之后不改变位置，比如 the child whom the nurse was looking after 不能写成 after+whom 形式。Which building did they blow up? 也不能写为 up+which 的形式。

三、介词的用法

介词后面一般紧跟宾语。这种宾语是名词或相当于名词的成分。一共有 11 种类型。

（1）介词+名词。例如：

I live in a small apartment. 我住在一个小的公寓里。

We are walking along the road. 我们顺着马路走。

（2）介词+代词。例如：

He talked to them. 他与他们讲话。

He is keen on it. 他热衷于这件事。

（3）介词+动名词。例如：

He learns English by watching English movies. 他通过看英文电影来学英语。

He preferred playing soccer to swimming. 他愿意踢足球而不愿去游泳。

（4）介词+不定式。例如：

He did nothing but/except play. 他什么也不做，只玩。

The solider would rather die than surrender. 这个士兵宁死不屈。

（不定式一般不能用作介词的宾语，只有在 but、except 和 than 后可以。这样用时 to 常常省略。）

（5）介词+疑问词+不定式。例如：

The issue of how to cope with the situation is a hot topic. 如何应付这种形势是大家热议的话题。

That depends on which method to apply. 这取决于使用哪种方法。

（6）介词+表示时间或地点的副词。例如：

He comes from abroad. 他来自外国。

He has been ill since last week. 自上周他就生病了。

（7）介词+形容词。例如：

In short, I have done my best. 总而言之，我尽力而为了。

At first, he failed; but at last, he succeeded. 开始的时候他失败了，但最终成功了。

（8）介词+介词短语。例如：

The moon emerged from behind the cloud. 月亮从云后面出现了。

He returned from beyond the sea. 他从海上归来。

（9）介词+that 引起的从句。例如：

I know nothing except that he is a trustworthy guy. 我只知道他是个可靠的人。

He is different from his brother in that he is quiet. 他与他的弟弟（哥哥）不同，他是个安静的人。

（10）介词+疑问词引起的从句。例如：

He does not care about who will be the new boss. 他不在乎谁会当新老板。

He wants to be informed of which position is the best for him. 他想知道哪个职位最适合他。

（11）介词+名词（代词）+介词短语。这种宾语通常跟在介词 with 后，表示伴随的情况。例如：

The teacher entered the classroom with a book under his arm. 老师胳膊下夹着一本书，走进了教室。

With his boss out of temper, he was worried. 他的老板发脾气了，他很担心。

四、表示时间和日期的介词 at, on, by, before, in

1. at, on

（1）用 at 来表示在某一时刻。例如：

at dawn 在黎明　　　　at six 在 6 点钟　　　　at 4：30 在 4 点 30 分

（2）用 at 来表示在 n 岁时。例如：

at sixteen/at the age of sixteen 16 岁的时候

（3）用 on 来表示在星期几或某日：

on Monday 在星期一　　　　on 6 June 在 6 月 6 日

（4）例外的情况。例如：

at night 在晚上

at Christmas/Easter 在圣诞节/复活节期间（不仅当天）

on the morning/afternoon/evening/night of (a certain date) 在某一具体日期的早上/下午/傍晚/夜里。例如：

We arrived in Beijing on the morning of the ninth. 我们在 9 号早上到达北京。

2. by, before

by a time/date/period＝at that time or before/not later than that date 在那一时刻/日期或不迟于那一日期

by+a time 常常和完成时态连用，尤其与将来完成时态连用。例如：

By the end of September I'll have read all those books. 到 9 月底我将已经把那些书全读完了。

3. in

in 表示月、年、世纪或更长的时间段。例如：

in May 在五月　　　　　　　in summer 在夏天　　　　　in 1990 在 1990 年

in the next century 在下个世纪　　in the Ice Age 在冰川时期

五、表示时间的介词 from，since，for，during

1. from，since 和 for

（1）from 通常和 to 或 till/until 连用。例如：

Most people work from nine to five. 大多数人从上午 9 点工作到下午 5 点。

from 也可以用于问地点。例如：

Where do you come from? 你是哪里人？

（2）since 只用于时间而从不用于地点之前，意指"从那时起到所指的时刻"。它常常和现在完成时或过去完成时连用。例如：

He has been here since Tuesday. 他从星期二开始一直在这里。（从星期二到现在）

since 也可以是时间连词。例如：

He has worked for them ever since he left school. 他离开学校以后就一直为他们工作。

（3）for 用来表示一段时间。例如：

for six years 六年之久　　　for two months 有两个月　　　for ever 永远

2. during 和 for

（1）during 用于已知的一段时间，包括大家熟知的节日，如 Christmas（圣诞节）、Easter（复活节），或者某种已确切限定的时期或阶段之前。例如：

during the Middle Ages 在中世纪　　　during my holidays 在我度假期间

涉及的行动可以持续于整个时期内或只发生在该时期中的某一时刻。例如：

It rained all Friday but stopped raining during the night. 星期五整天都在下雨，但夜里雨停了。（在某一时刻）

（2）for（表示目的）可以用于已知的时间阶段之前。例如：

I went there/I hired a car/I rented a house for my holidays/for the summer. 为了度假/过夏天我到了那里/我租了一辆汽车/我租了一所房子。

六、表示时间的介词 to，till/until，after

1. to 和 till/until

（1）to 可以用于时间和地点之前；till/until 只用于时间之前。可以用 from...to 或 from...till/until 的结构。例如：

They worked from five to ten/from five till ten. 他们从 5 点工作到 10 点。（注意：勿与 at five to ten 混淆，其意为 9 点 55 分。）

但如果句中没有 from，就要用 till/until 而不用 to。例如：

Let's start now and work till dark. 让我们现在开始工作一直到天黑。（这里不能用 to。）

（2）till/until 常常和否定意义的动词连用，以表示强调时间晚了。例如：

We didn't get home till 1 a.m. 我们一直到凌晨一点钟才到家。

He usually pays me on Friday but last week he didn't pay me till the following Monday. 他一般在星期五付给我钱，但上星期他一直到第二周的星期一才把钱给我。

2. after, afterwards（副词）

（1）after 是介词，后面必须接名词、代词或动名词。例如：

Don't bathe immediately after a meal/after eating.

Don't have a meal and bathe immediately after it. 不要就餐之后立即游泳。

（2）如果不想名词、代词或动名词，就不能用 after，但可以用 afterwards（=after that）或者 then。例如：

Don't have a meal and bathe immediately afterwards. 不要饭后立即游泳。

They bathed and afterwards played game/played games afterwards.

They bathed and then played games. 他们游泳，然后做游戏。

afterwards 可以位于句首或句末，并且可以由 soon, immediate（ly），not long 等修饰。例如：

Soon afterwards we got a letter.

We got a letter not long afterwards. 不久之后我们收到了一封信。

七、表示移动和运动的介词 from, to, at, in, by, on, into, onto, off, out, out of

（1）可以说从（from）出发地前往（to）目的地。例如：

They flew/drove/cycled/walked from Paris to Rome. 他们从巴黎乘飞机/驾车/骑车/步行前往罗马。

（2）表示"到达"的意思可以用 arrive at/in, get to, reach（不用介词）。可以说到达（arrive in）一个城市或国家；到达（arrive at/in）一个村庄；到达（arrive at）任何其他目的地。例如：

They arrived in Spain/in Madrid. 他们到达西班牙/马德里。

I arrived at the hotel/at the airport /at the bridge/at the crossroads. 我到了旅馆/飞机场/桥梁/十字路口。

（3）表示运输方法的介词有 by, on, get in/into/on/onto/off/out of。可以说乘汽车旅行（travel by car 或者 in the/my/Tom's car）。

表示旅行的方式还有：乘公共汽车（by bus）、乘火车（by train），乘飞机（by plane/by air），乘直升机（by helicopter），乘船（by sea），乘气垫船（by hovercraft）等。

旅行时还可以经由一定路线（by a certain route）或经由某一地点（by a certain place，尽管 via 更为常用）。例如：

We went by the M4. 我们经 M4 路线前往。

We went via Reading. 我们经里丁前往。

（4）当进出某些建筑物、公共机构、国家等并不容易时，也可用 get in/into/out/out of 来表示进出这些地方，而不用 go/come/return 等词。in 和 out 在这些地方作副词用。例如：

I've lost my keys! How are we going to get into the flat/to get in?（in 为副词）我把钥匙丢了！我们怎么进屋/进去呢？

The house is on fire! We had better get out!（out 为副词）房子着火了！我们最好出去！

It's difficult to get into a university nowadays. 如今进大学读书是难事。

八、表示位置的介词 above, over, under, below, beneath 等

1. above, over

above（介词和副词）和 over（介词）两者的含义都是 higher than（高于），有时可以互换使用。例如：

The helicopter hovered above/over us. 直升机在我们的上空盘旋。

但 over 还可以表示覆盖（covering）、在对面（on the other side of）、横过（across）、从

一边到另一边（from one side to the other）。例如：

　　We put a rug over him. 我们往他身上盖了一块小毛毯。

　　He lives over the mountain. 他住在山的那一边。

　2. below, under

　　below（介词和副词）和 under（介词）两者的含义都是 lower than（低于），有时可以互换使用，但 under 可以表示 contact（接触）。例如：

　　She put the letter under the pillow. 她把信放在枕头下。

　3. beneath

　　有时 beneath 可代替 under，但它表示抽象含义，而不表示具体的位置下。例如：

　　He would think it beneath him to tell a lie. 他认为说谎有失于他的身份。

　　She married beneath her. 她嫁给了一位社会地位比她低的人。（进了较低的社会阶层）

　4. beside, between, behind, in front of, opposite

　　这几个介词的用法如下：

　　Tom is beside Ann; Mary is beside Bob, etc. 汤姆在安旁边；玛丽在鲍勃旁边（依此类推）。

　　Ann is between Tom and Bill; Bob is between Mary and Jane. 安在汤姆和比尔之间；鲍勃在玛丽和珍妮之间。

　　Mary is behind Tom; Tom is in front of Mary. 玛丽在汤姆后面；汤姆在玛丽前面。

　　但是，如果汤姆和玛丽正在吃饭，汤姆坐在桌子的一边，玛丽坐在另一边，我们就不用 in front of，而说：

　　Tom is sitting opposite Mary. 汤姆坐在玛丽对面。

　　Tom is facing Mary. 汤姆面向玛丽。

　　He stood in front of me（他站在我的前面）既可以指 He stood with his back to me（他背朝我站着），也可以指 He faced me（他面向着我）。

　　住在街道一边的人说街道另一边的房子时用 the houses opposite us（我们对面的房子），而不说 the houses in front of us（在我们前面的房子）。

　5. between, among

　　（1）between 常常表示一个人或物与其他两个人或物之间的关系。但是，当我们心目中已有了一个确定的数字，between 也可以用来表示在更多的人或物之间。例如：

　　Luxemburg lies between Belgium, Germany and France. 卢森堡位于比利时、德国和法国之间。

　　（2）among 表示一个人或物与其他两个以上的人或物间的关系，在正常情况下我们心目中并无确定的数目。例如：

　　He was happy to be among his friends again. 他很高兴又回到朋友们中来了。

　　a village among the hills 一个群山环绕的村庄

　　九、but, except

　　这两个介词具有同样的意思，并且可以互换使用。

　　（1）but 更常用在"介词+宾语"结构中。在句子中直接跟在 nobody（没人）/none（没有任何人或事物）/nothing（什么也没有）/nowhere（什么地方也不）等之后。例如：

Nobody but Tom knew the way. 只有汤姆认得路。

Nothing but the best is sold in our shop. 本店所售商品均属精品。

（2）句子中介词短语位于较后的位置时，常用 except。例如：

Nobody knew the way except Tom.

（3）在 all（全体，一切）/everybody（大家，人人，每人）/everyone（每一个人）/everything（每一件事）/everywhere（各个地方）等之后，常用 except。在 anybody（任何人）/anything（任何事）/anywhere（任何地方）等之后，but 比 except 更表示强调。例如：

You can park anywhere but/except here. 你在哪儿停车都行，就是不能在这里停放车子。

（4）but 和 except 后面还可跟不带 to 的动词不定式。

练 习

I. 选择题。

1. The English teacher is writing _____ a piece of chalk on the blackboard while the students are writing _____ ink in exercise books.
   A. with, in   B. in, with   C. in, in   D. with, with

2. The worker can make chairs _____ wood, and also can make paper _____ wood.
   A. from, of   B. of, from   C. of, of   D. from, from

3. Mary dropped in _____ Mr. Smith, but he was not at home, so she went to drop in _____ Mr. Smith's office.
   A. on, on   B. at, at   C. on, at   D. at, on

4. The teacher is not only strict _____ his pupils but also strict _____ his own work.
   A. with, with   B. in, in   C. in, with   D. with, in

5. His grandfather died _____ the wound that the enemy soldier had given him, and then his grandmother died _____ hungry and cold.
   A. from, of   B. of, from   C. from, from   D. of, of

6. If you run _____ two hares you will catch neither.
   A. into   B. after   C. off   D. out of

7. This is a common mistake _____ students.
   A. between   B. over   C. among   D. about

8. My father began to work _____ a bus driver when he was twenty years old.
   A. for   B. to   C. at   D. as

9. _____ hearing the news, I was wild _____ joy.
   A. At, in   B. On, with   C. After, by   D. /, over

10. I don't think Xiao Li is _____ the other students _____ mathematics.
    A. after, on   B. after, with   C. behind, in   D. behind, at

11. Nobody knows it _____ me.

A. except for B. except that C. besides D. but

12. The window is never opened _____ in summer.

    A. but B. except C. except for D. but for

13. It happened _____ the Long March.

    A. during B. in C. at D. for

14. We go to school _____ a bike.

    A. in B. on C. by D. over

15. It's very kind _____ you to repair the bike _____ me.

    A. for, for B. of, of C. of, for D. for, of

16. Fresh air is good _____ your health.

    A. at B. for C. of D. to

17. The boy is waiting _____ his sister and they will go to the hospital to wait _____ their sick mother.

    A. for, on B. on, for C. for, for D. on, on

18. The group is made up _____ five students. And they are studying hard to make up _____ the lost time.

    A. of, of B. for, for C. of, for D. for, of

19. The PLA man saved the boy _____ death.

    A. of B. from C. to D. on

20. He will come _____ three days.

    A. before B. after C. in D. later

Ⅱ. 用合适的介词填空。

1. The driver informing us _____ the accident quitted his job a week later.

2. We are not supposed _____ play football on Sundays.

3. We cannot figure _____ why quite a number of insects, birds, and animals are dying out.

4. Janet has a large collection _____ foreign coins; she loves showing them off to every visitor.

5. I don't think you will have any difficulty _____ passing this exam.

6. We should be loyal _____ our country.

7. I have been _____ good terms with my classmates.

8. We congratulated you _____ winning the contest.

9. To make full use _____ the land, two or more crops are planted each year where possible.

10. People make us laugh by making fun _____ somebody's way of dressing or telling an amusing story.

Unit 7

 Part Seven　　Writing

Invitation Card

Directions：In this part, you are going to learn how to write an *Invitation Card* and then try your hand.

1. Read the following sample.

> Dec. 21st
>
> Dear Prof. Stanley,
>
> 　　The New Year is around the corner. We, all the international students and teachers at the International College, will hold a dancing party at the dining hall of the 2nd floor from 7：00 to 10：00 this Friday evening (Dec. 29th). Would you and Mrs. Stanley come and join us? We are looking forward to your arrival.
>
> 　　　　　　　　　　　　　　　　　　　　　　　　　　　　　Yours sincerely,
> 　　　　　　　　　　　　　　　　　　　　　　　　　　　　　　　Li Hui

2. Translate the following schedule into English.

> 尊敬的戴维先生：
>
> 　　圣诞节就要到了，我们系将于本周五（12月24日）晚7点在学生活动中心举行英语晚会。希望您和太太能和我们一起享受晚会的乐趣。我们热切期望您的光临！
>
> 　　　　　　　　　　　　　　　　　　　　　　　　　　　　　　诚挚的
> 　　　　　　　　　　　　　　　　　　　　　　　　　　　　　　　肖玉
> 　　　　　　　　　　　　　　　　　　　　　　　　　　　　　　12月19日

Data Bank

1. We are having a tea party/get-together/an English Evening at the hall at 7：00 p.m. on...
   我们将于×日晚7点在礼堂举行茶话会/聚会/英语晚会。

2. I wonder if you would be able to join us for dinner tomorrow evening.
   我想知道明天晚上你是否能来参加晚宴。

3. Would you like to come to our dinner party on Saturday evening?
   星期六晚上你能否来参加晚宴？

4. We would be very glad if you could come.
   如能光临，我们会非常高兴。

5. We are looking forward to your coming/arrival.

我们期待着你的到来。

Tips

普通的请帖，一般采用便条的形式，书写格式与普通书信相近。普通请帖虽不及正式请柬庄重，却也不失大方，能让熟悉且亲近的朋友产生亲切、随和的感觉，所以同样可用于宴会甚至婚礼等场合。在内容方面，一定要写清下列几点：

（1）邀请对象；

（2）活动时间、地点、安排以及其他注意事项；

（3）表达盼望被邀请人能如期参加的愿望。

Culture Notes

1. MySpace: a social networking website. Its headquarters are in Beverly Hills, California, US. MySpace became the most popular social networking site in the United States in June 2006.

2. Amazon Inc.: an American-based multinational electronic commerce company. Headquartered in Seattle, Washington, it is America's largest online retailer.

Unit 8

Entertainment

 Part One Warm-up

1. Think of terms about types of TV programs and put them in the following box.

2. What is your favorite TV channel? Give your reasons.
3. What is your favorite cartoon? Why do you like it?
4. Can you tell the names of some cartoon characters?

Part Two Speaking and Listening

Section A Listen to the following conversation and then repeat.

Tom: Did you see the movie on channel 6 last night? It is quite interesting.

Susan: No. I missed it. I went shopping for clothes.

Tom: What a pity! It was an excellent film. It had been made especially for television, you know.

Susan: Oh, I see. But last night Mary called me to go shopping with her. So I went.

Tom: You remember that the critic thought that it was one of the best films of the last ten years.

Susan: Yes. I do remember. He felt it would be a candidate for some film awards at the end of the year.

Tom: Well, I can't agree more. I haven't seen such a marvelous plot and such fantastic acting in a long time!

Susan: Sounds as if I'll have to see it, if they ever re-run it.

Section B Listen to the following short passage and fill in the missing words.

Michael Jackson's doctor is planning to 1) _____ to police in Los Angeles on Friday morning. After Michael's death, it is expected he will be 2) _____ over the singer's death. According to reports, Dr. Conrad Murray will turn himself into police before he is taken to 3) _____ to face a judge later that day. Prosecutors (检察官) have 4) _____ to say whether they will charge Dr. Murray with 5) _____ or not.

Part Three Detailed Reading

Unit 8

The Creator of "Peanuts"

Millions of people around the world who loved the comic strip "Peanuts" were sad when Charles Schulz died in February, 2000. He was seventy-seven years old. The artist who created Charlie Brown and his dog Snoopy had retired a month earlier because of poor health.

Charles Schulz drew "Peanuts" for fifty years and brought happiness to millions of people. The comic strip first appeared in seven American newspapers in 1950. At that time, the subjects were all children and animals. They still are. People love these characters because they demonstrate the failings and strengths of all human beings. For example, Charlie Brown is nervous and lacks self-confidence, who usually cannot get things right. He is even unable to fly a kite, win a baseball game or kick a football. But he tries his best, and never stops trying.

Charlie Brown has a dog named Snoopy who may be even more popular than Charlie. Snoopy is a funny character. He is always trying to write the great American novel, but cannot get beyond the first line of his book. He writes "It was a dark and stormy night" again and again. There are other memorable characters in the "Peanuts" comic strip. Lucy mistrusts everyone. Schroeder plays a small toy piano, and every year celebrates the birthday of composer Ludwig von Beethoven. Linus always carries a blanket to feel secure. Peppermint Patty is good at sports, who likes Charlie Brown very much.

Charles Schulz said he saw himself in some of his characters. He recognized himself in Charlie Brown's continued failures, in Snoopy's humor, in Lucy's moments of anger, and in the insecure feelings of Linus. Some of the situations in "Peanuts" seem to have developed from Mr. Schulz's own life experiences.

Over the years Mr. Schulz drew about eighteen thousand comic strips without any help. This is very unusual for a comic strip artist. Charles Schulz also wrote the stories for the television and film productions of "Peanuts." There have been more than fifty animated television shows based on "Peanuts." Charles Schulz's comic strip created a whole industry. There are "Peanuts" toys, videos, clothes and greeting cards.

In 2002, a new museum opened in Santa Rosa, California. It celebrates the life and work of the creator of "Peanuts," which provides a place where people can see the first drawings of all his comic strips and learn about his work. One area of the museum re-creates the room where Charles Schulz drew his cartoons. Another area shows things from his childhood and awards he received. His wife wanted the museum to show not only his work, but also how he lived. The museum also shows works by other artists that honor "Peanuts."

(This text is adapted from the article *People in America — Charles Schulz* on the website www.unsv.com, 2011-12-17.)

New Words

creator	[kriˈeitə]	n.	a person who creates; originator 创造者，创作者
comic	[ˈkɔmik]	n.	a book or magazine containing comic strips 连环漫画，连环画册
strip	[strip]	n.	a sequence of drawings telling a story in a newspaper or comic book 连环漫画
retire	[riˈtaiə]	n./v.	to stop performing one's work or with draw from one's position 退休，退职
subject	[ˈsʌbdʒikt]	n.	some situation or event that is thought about 主题，话题，题材
character	[ˈkæriktə]	n.	an imaginary person represented in a work of fiction (play/film/story) 人物
demonstrate	[ˈdemənstreit]	v.	to show or prove something clearly 示范，演示，证明
failing	[ˈfeiliŋ]	n.	a flaw or weak point 失败，缺点，过失
nervous	[ˈnəːvəs]	adj.	causing or fraught with or showing anxiety. 神经紧张的，不安的
lack	[læk]	v.	to be without 缺乏，不足
self-confidence	[selfˈkɔnfidəns]	n.	belief in yourself and your abilities 自信
popular	[ˈpɔpjulə]	adj.	regarded with great favor, approval or affection, especially by the general public 大众的，流行的
novel	[ˈnɔvəl]	n.	a extended fictional work in prose, usually in the form of a story 小说
line	[lain]	n.	text consisting of a row of words written across a page or computer screen (诗文的) 一行
mistrust	[misˈtrʌst]	v.	to have doubts or suspicions about somebody or something 不信任
celebrate	[ˈselibreit]	v.	to observe (a birthday, anniversary, etc.) 庆祝，祝贺
composer	[kəmˈpəuzə]	n.	a person who composes music 创作者（尤指乐曲）
secure	[siˈkjuə]	adj.	free from danger or risk 安心的，安全的
humor	[ˈhjuːmə]	n.	the quality of being funny 幽默，诙谐
unusual	[ʌnˈjuːʒuəl]	adj.	out of the ordinary; uncommon; extraordinary 不平常的，异常的
animated	[ˈæniˌmeitid]	adj.	producing in the form of cartons (影片等) 以动画形式制作的
award	[əˈwɔːd]	n.	something given for victory or superiority in a contest or competition or for winning a lottery 奖，奖品
honor	[ˈɔnə]	v.	show respect towards somebody 尊敬

Unit 8

Phrases & Expressions

base on: to use an idea, a fact, a situation, etc. as the point from which something can be developed 基于，以……为依据

例：This novel is based on historical facts. 这部小说是以历史事实为根据的。

Comprehension of the Text

Choose the best answer for each of the following questions.

1. Which of the following is TRUE according to the passage? _____
   A. Charles Schulz drew "Peanuts" for 77 years.
   B. Charlie Brown is more popular than his dog.
   C. Some situations in "Peanuts" are similar with Charles Schulz's life experience.
   D. Many people help Mr. Schulz draw about eighteen thousand comic strips.

2. Which of the following words can describe Snoopy according to the passage? _____
   A. Funny and nervous.
   B. Nervous and humorous.
   C. Humorous and insecure.
   D. Funny and humorous.

3. How many characters in "Peanuts" are mentioned in the passage? _____
   A. 4.   B. 5.   C. 6.   D. 7.

4. Which is not included in the industry that Charles Schulz's comic strip created? _____
   A. "Peanuts" toys.
   B. "Peanuts" music.
   C. "Peanuts" videos.
   D. "Peanuts" clothes and greeting cards.

5. What can't people see in the new museum opened in 2002 in Santa Rosa, California? _____
   A. The first drawings of all Charles Schulz's comic strips.
   B. Works by other artists that honor "Peanuts".
   C. Things from Charles Schulz's childhood and awards he received.
   D. Works by composer Ludwig von Beethoven.

137

Part Four Exercises

Task 1 Choose the definition from Column B that best matches each word or phrase in Column A.

A	B
1. character	a. to show or prove something clearly
2. composer	b. be without
3. honor	c. a person who creates; originator
4. self-confidence	d. an imaginary person represented in a work of fiction
5. memorable	e. to have doubts or suspicions about somebody or something
6. unusual	f. show respect towards somebody
7. lack	g. a person who composes music
8. creator	h. worth remembering
9. mistrust	i. belief in yourself and your abilities
10. demonstrate	j. out of the ordinary; uncommon; extraordinary

Task 2 Fill in the blanks with the words or expressions given below. Change the form where necessary.

composer	retire	popular	humor	demonstrate
base on	celebrate	lack	memorable	character

1. We went to the church to _____ Christmas Eve.
2. Baseball is more _____ than any other sport in Japan.
3. The film was _____ for its fine acting.
4. I will now _____ how the machine works.
5. Their relationship was _____ mutual respect.
6. My father _____ at the age of 60.
7. Candida is the most interesting _____ in the play.
8. Unlike his brother, he has a good sense of _____.
9. Beethoven, Mozart are great classical music _____.
10. He is good at his job but he seems to _____ confidence.

138

Task 3 Translate the following sentences into English, paying special attention to the underlined parts.

1. 她不相信自己有开车的能力。(mistrust)
2. 那个梯子安全吗?(secure)
3. 他们开了一瓶酒来庆祝他的成功。(celebrate)
4. 有什么不平常的事发生了吗?(unusual)
5. 孩子们应该尊敬父母。(honor)

Part Five   Supplementary Reading

The Barbie Doll

In the early 1950s, Handler saw that her young daughter, Barbara, and her girlfriends enjoyed playing with adult female dolls as much as or more than with baby dolls. Handler felt that it was just as important for girls to imagine what they themselves might grow up to become as it was for them to focus on what caring for children might be like.

Because all the adult dolls then available were made of paper or cardboard, Handler decided to create a three-dimensional adult female doll for her daughter. Handler took her idea to the ad executives at Mattel Corp., the company that she and her husband, Elliot, had founded in their garage some years before: the committee (all-male) rejected the idea as too expensive, and with little potential for wide market appeal.

Soon after, Handler returned from a trip to Europe with a "Lilli" doll, modeled after a character in a German comic strip. Handler spent some time designing a doll similar to Lilli, and the result was the Barbie doll (named in honor of the Handlers' daughter), a small model of the "girl next door".

Mattel finally agreed to back Handler's efforts. Later Barbie set a new sales record for Mattel its first year on the market (351,000 dolls, at $3 each). Today, with over one billion dolls sold, the Barbie product line is the most successful in the history of the toy industry.

The Barbie doll has been joined by friends and family over the years, including the Ken doll — named for the Handlers' son — in 1961, Midge in 1963, Skipper in 1965 and Christie — an African-American doll — in 1968. More recently, in 1995, the Barbie doll gained a little sister, Baby Sister Kelly, and, in 1997, a disabled friend in a wheelchair, Share a Smile Becky.

The world of the Barbie doll today is a great deal more than a doll. Barbie doll is allowing girls to use their computers to design, create, play and dream using Barbie software. The Barbie line has also developed into many exciting products for girls, including books, clothes, food, home furniture and home electronics.

Playing with Barbie dolls seems as a rule to improve girls' self-image and expand their sense of their potential rather than the opposite. This has become more true over the years, as Barbie herself has expanded her horizons: she has now appeared as a doctor, firefighter, astronaut, businesswoman, police officer, and athlete. Over the years, Barbie has achieved the title of the most popular fashion doll ever created.

(This text is adapted from http://www.ideafinder.com/history/inventions/barbiedoll.htm, 2011-12-20.)

New Words

doll	[dɔl]	n.	toy 玩偶,（玩具）娃娃
female	[ˈfiːmeil]	adj.	being a woman or a girl 雌的, 女（性）的
focus	[ˈfəukəs]	v.	direct one's attention on something （使）集中, 聚集
available	[əˈveiləbl]	adj.	ready for use or service 可用的, 可得到的, 有用的
cardboard	[ˈkɑːdbɔːd]	n.	a stiff moderately thick paper 厚纸板
three-dimensional	[ˈθriːdiˈmenʃənəl]	adj.	involving or relating to three dimensions or aspects 三维的, 三度的, 立体的, 生动的
executive	[igˈzekjutiv]	n.	a person or a group of people responsible for the administration of a company or an organization 执行者, 主管; 行政部门
garage	[ˈgɑrɑːʒ]	n.	a building for keeping the car in, usually next to or attached to a house 车库
committee	[kəˈmiti]	n.	a special group delegated to consider some matter 委员会

appeal	[əˈpiːl]	n.	attractiveness that interests, pleases somebody or stimulates 吸引力
design	[diˈzain]	v.	to make a drawing or plan of something that will be made or built 计划，设计
back	[bæk]	v.	to give support or one's approval to somebody or something 支持
wheelchair	[ˈwiːlˌtʃɛə]	n.	a chair with wheels, used by people who cannot walk 轮椅
furniture	[ˈfəːnitʃə]	n.	objects that can be moved, such as tables, chairs and beds, that are put into a house or an office to make it suitable for living or working in 家具
expand	[iksˈpænd]	v.	to become larger in size, number, or amount 增加，扩展，使……膨胀
horizon	[həˈraizn]	n.	the limit of your ideas, knowledge, and experience 视野，眼界
firefighter	[ˈfaiəˌfaitə]	n.	a member of a fire department who tries to extinguish fires 消防队员
astronaut	[ˈæstrənɔːt]	n.	a person trained to travel in a spacecraft 宇航员
athlete	[ˈæθliːt]	n.	a person trained to compete in sports 运动员

Phrases & Expressions

1. focus on: center upon 集中在……
   例：Today we're going to focus on the question of homeless people. 今天，我们主要讨论无家可归者的问题。
2. in honor of: in order to show respect and admiration for somebody or something 为纪念，为向……表示敬意，为……庆祝
   例：The monument is in honor of a scientist. 那座纪念碑是为纪念一位科学家而建的。

Comprehension of the Text

Answer the following questions according to the text.

1. Why did the committee reject Handler's idea of creating a three-dimensional adult female doll?
2. How was the Barbie doll first created?
3. What advantages can Barbie's dolls bring to a girl?

Part Six Grammar

连词（Conjunctions）

连词是一种虚词，用于连接单词、短语、从句或句子，在句子中不单独作句子成分。从形式上看，连词可以分为如下几类：

（1）简单连词，如：and，but，if；
（2）副词连词，如：then，besides，still；
（3）短语连词，如：or rather，on the other hand；
（4）关联连词，如：so...that...，either...or...，not only...but...。

按其性质又可分为并列连词和从属连词。

并列连词用于连接并列的单词、短语、从句或句子，如：and，but，or，nor，so，therefore，yet，however，for，hence，as well as，both...and，not only...but also，either...or，neither...nor，(and) then 等。

从属连词主要引出名词性从句（主语从句、宾语从句、表语从句等）和状语从句（时间状语从句、条件状语从句、目的状语从句等），引出名词性从句的连词如 that，whether 等，引出状语从句的连词如 when，because，since，if 等。

一、并列连词的用法

1. 表示转折关系

这类连词主要有 but，yet 等。例如：

Someone told me the accident, but I don't remember who. 有人给我讲了那个事故，但我不记得是谁了。

He said he would be supportive, yet he would not offer any help. 他说他会支持我们，但却不肯帮助我们。

2. 表示因果关系

这类连词主要有 for，so 等。例如：

The student did not study hard, so he failed in the final exam. 这个学生学习不用功，所以期末考试没过。

He shook his head, for he thought differently. 他摇摇头，因为他的想法与此不同。

注意：for 表示原因通常不能放句首，也不能单独使用。

3. 表示并列关系

这类连词主要有 and，or，either...or，neither...nor，not only...but (also)，both...and，as well as 等。例如：

He can't swim and she can't swim either. 他不会游泳，她也不会。

Not only did the dog bark at him, but (it) bit him. 这只狗不但对他叫，而且咬了他。

Neither dad nor mum is at home today. 今天父母都不在家。

二、从属连词的用法

1. 引导时间状语从句

（1）表示"当……时候"或"每当"。这类连词主要有 when, while, as, whenever。例如：

Don't lose hope when you are in trouble. 陷入麻烦当中时不要失去希望。

Mom is doing dishes while father is reading newspaper. 妈妈在洗碗，爸爸在看报纸。

（2）表示"在……之前（或之后）"。这类连词主要有 before, after。例如：

Remember to turn off the light before you leave. 离开前把灯关掉。

I'll leave after he comes back. 他回来后我就走。

（3）表示"自从"或"直到"。这类连词主要有 since, until, till。例如：

The little girl has been playing the piano since she was four. 这个小女孩四岁开始弹琴。

Never trouble trouble till trouble troubles you. （谚）不要无事惹事。

（4）表示"一……就"。这类连词主要有 as soon as, the moment, the minute, the second, the instant, immediately, directly, instantly, once, no sooner…than, hardly…when 等。例如：

I arranged the flowers in the vase as soon as I came back home. 一回到家里，我就把花在花瓶里插好。

The moment I arrive, I'll give you a call. 我一到达就给你打电话。

Once you make up your mind, you must continue. 你一旦下定决心，就一定要坚持。

（5）表示"上次""下次""每次"等。这类连词主要有 every time（每次），each time（每次），(the) next time（下次），any time（随时），(the) last time（上次），the first time（第一次）。例如：

We became good friends the first time we met at a party. 我们第一次在舞会上认识后就成了好朋友。

You can come to me any time you are in trouble. 你遇到麻烦的话，可以随时来找我。

注意：every time, each time, any time 前不用冠词，(the) next time, (the) last time 中的冠词可以省略，而 the first time 中的冠词通常不能省略。

2. 引导条件状语从句

这类连词主要有 if, unless, as (so) long as 等。例如：

Do you mind if I turn down the music? 我把音乐声调小一点儿，你不介意吧？

As long as you admit your mistake, he will forgive you. 只要你承认错误，他会原谅你的。

3. 引导目的状语从句

这类连词主要有 in order that, so that, in case, for fear 等。例如：

The students did so well in the exam that the teacher was pleased with them. 学生考试考得很好，老师对他们很满意。

You'd better take an umbrella in case it rains. 你最好带把伞，以防下雨。

I lent her my car in order that she could save time. 我把车借给她，以便她能节省一些时间。

4. 引导结果状语从句

这类连词主要有 so that, so…that, such…that 等。例如：

I went to the classroom early so that I got a front seat. 我去教室很早，所以找到了一个前排座位。

I have so many friends that I feel happy all the time. 我有很多朋友，所以一直觉得很幸福。

He is such a hard-working man that he achieved great success. 他很努力，所以取得了巨大成功。

5. 引导原因状语从句

这类连词主要有 because, as, since, seeing (that), now (that), considering (that) 等。例如：

The teacher scolded him because he was late again. 因为他又迟到了，老师责备了他。

Seeing that he is just a child, we can forgive him. 鉴于他还是个孩子，我们应该原谅他。

Now that you are an adult, you should take responsibility for yourself. 既然你已经是成人了，就应该对自己负责任了。

6. 引导让步状语从句

这类连词主要有 although, though, even though, even if, while, however, whatever, whoever, whenever, wherever 等。例如：

Although they come from different backgrounds, they are good friends. 他们虽然有完全不同的背景，却成了好朋友。

He carried out the plan even though nobody agreed with him. 即使没人同意，他还是执行了该计划。

Whatever you choose, I will always be there for you. 不管你做什么选择，我都支持你。

7. 引导方式状语从句

这类连词主要有 as, as if, as though, the way 等。例如：

You can operate the machine as the instruction tells you to. 你可以按照说明书上说的那样来操作机器。

He talks as if he had been there when the accident happened. 他说起话来好像他当时就在事发现场。

I am moved by the way he treats me. 他对我很好，我很感动。

8. 引导地点状语从句

这类连词主要有 where, wherever, everywhere, anywhere 等。例如：

This is the house where the writer had lived all his life. 这就是这个作家一生一直居住的房子。

I'll follow you wherever you go. 我会跟随你到天涯海角。

Everywhere I go, I make friends. 不管我走到哪里，我都结识新朋友。

9. 引导比较状语从句

这类连词主要有 than 和 as...as。例如：

His twin brother is taller than he is. 他的双胞胎弟弟（哥哥）比他个高。

You should keep the room as clean as your brother's. 你应该把你的房间收拾得像你哥哥（弟弟）的房间一样整洁。

Unit 8

10. 引导名词性从句

这类连词主要有 that, whether, if 等，它们用于引导主语从句、表语从句、宾语从句和同位语从句。其中 that 不仅不充当句子成分，而且没有词义，在句子中只起连接作用；if, whether 虽不充当句子成分，但有词义，表示"是否"。例如：

That he is an orphan makes us feel sorry for him. 他是个孤儿，我们都很同情他。

I wonder if what he said is true. 我怀疑他说的话的真实性。

They don't care whether my reports are good or bad. 他们不关心我的报告质量的好坏。

练 习

I. 选择题。

1. I'd get it for you _____ I could remember who last borrowed the book.
   A. on condition that   B. now that
   C. except that   D. considering that

2. The robber told him that he had better keep silent _____ he wanted to get into trouble.
   A. if   B. unless   C. otherwise   D. whether

3. Strange _____ his behavior may be, there is a very good reason for it.
   A. although   B. even if   C. that   D. as

4. We are worried about our son because no one is aware _____ he has gone.
   A. the place   B. of where   C. about the place D. where

5. The professor spoke in a loud voice _____ every one of us could hear him.
   A. such that   B. so   C. so that   D. such

6. When he just got off the plane, he gave us a good description of _____ in Spain.
   A. what he had seen   B. that he had seen
   C. which he had seen   D. he had seen what

7. It is fitted with a small transformer, by means of _____ the voltage of the currency can be adjusted.
   A. whom   B. which   C. what   D. that

8. I don't know why she's looking at me _____ she knew me. I've never seen her before in my life.
   A. as   B. although   C. even if   D. as if

9. No sooner had he finished his speech _____ stormy applause broke out.
   A. when   B. then   C. than   D. as

10. It is hard to avoid mistakes. _____ you correct them conscientiously, it will be all right.
    A. In the case B. As long as C. Although   D. Despite

11. Geometry, _____ I know nothing, seems a very dull subject.
    A. that   B. about that C. which   D. about which

145

12. The highest temperature _____ in any furnace on earth is about 10,000 centigrade.
    A. we can get   B. that we can get it
    C. which we can get it D. what we can get
13. We sent the horses to a considerable distance, _____ they should disturb the children.
    A. less   B. lest   C. last   D. least
14. Sound is conducted through steel in the same manner _____.
    A. as in air   B. as through air   C. as air does   D. like air
15. _____ he was putting on his uniform, the officer found that one of the sleeves was torn.
    A. Since   B. Unless   C. As   D. Before
16. The police finally caught up with the man _____ was the escaped prisoner.
    A. who they thought   B. whom they thought
    C. they thought him   D. that they thought him
17. _____ knows the name of this song will receive a prize from the radio station.
    A. Whoever   B. Those
    C. Whichever people   D. Any people
18. _____ do you believe is not about to support our plan?
    A. Whom   B. Who   C. Whomever   D. Which
19. He didn't know French, _____ made it difficult for him to study at a university in France.
    A. that   B. as   C. this   D. which
20. She is a fine singer, _____ her mother used to be.
    A. like   B. that   C. as   D. which

II. 用合适的词填空。

1. The fact is _____ I have lost interest in the book.
2. Go and get your coat. It's _____ you left it.
3. I wonder _____ you are getting on with your studies.
4. The question is _____ can complete the difficult task.
5. He got caught in the heavy traffic. That was _____ he was late.
6. _____ leaves the room last ought to turn off the light.
7. _____ you have done might do harm to others.
8. The moment _____ I saw you, I recognized you.
9. For a person with reading habits, a printed page contains not only words _____ ideas, thoughts and feelings.
10. Information technology is taught in most schools, _____ we have entered the information society.

Thank-you Note

Directions: In this part, you are going to learn how to write a *Thank-you Note* and then try your hand.

1. Read the following sample.

> Jan. 6, 2011
>
> Dear Lili,
>
> Many thanks for your warm invitation to your birthday party at the weekend. It's an unforgettable weekend for me. I can't remember when I have had a more pleasant and relaxing time. I really appreciate your hospitality.
>
> Yours faithfully,
> Lanlan

2. Translate the following thank-you note into English.

> 亲爱的弗兰克夫妇：
>
> 　　非常感谢你们热情邀请我参加你们的结婚 10 周年纪念宴会。宴会的温情、浪漫气氛深深打动了我，给我留下了难以忘怀的印象。我十分羡慕你们夫妇，并由衷地祝福你们幸福长久。
>
> 　　十分感谢你们的盛情。
>
> 你诚挚的，
> 张磊
> 2010 年 2 月 15 日

Data Bank

1. Please accept（I wish to express） my sincere（grateful/profound）appreciation for…
   请接受（致以）真挚的（衷心的/深切的）感谢……

2. I sincerely（deeply/warmly）appreciate …
   我真挚地（深深地/热情地）感谢……

3. I am very sincerely（most/truly）grateful to you for…
   为了……，我非常真挚地（深深地/真诚地）感谢您。

4. It was good（fine/charming/thoughtful）of you…

承蒙好意（美意/盛情/关心）……

5. It's generous of you to take so much interest in my work（to give me so much of your time/to show me so much consideration）.
承蒙对我的工作如此操心（为我花费这么多时间/对我如此关怀）。

6. We are indebted to you…
我们感谢你……

7. I regret very much that I did not have an opportunity to thank you personally for…
未能面谢，深表遗憾。

Tips

　　在英语国家，接受了朋友的礼物、招待、慰问和祝贺之后，写封感谢信是很常见的事情。这种感谢信的语言简洁明了，形式介乎于信件和便条之间，并没有一成不变的格式，但要写得及时，写得真挚动人。一般来说，最好在接受礼物或款待之后的两至三天内写给朋友。

Test Paper 2

Part I Listening Comprehension (15 minutes)

Directions: This part is to test your listening ability. It consists of 3 sections.

Section A

Directions: This section is to test your ability to give proper answers to questions. There are 5 recorded questions in it. After each question, there is a pause. The questions will be spoken two times. When you hear a question, you should decide on the correct answer from the 4 choices marked A), B), C) and D) given in your test paper. Then you should mark the corresponding letter on the Answer Sheet with a single line through the centre.

Example:

You will hear: I wonder if you could give Mr. Wang a message for me?

You will read: A) I'm not sure.

　　　　　　　B) You're right.

　　　　　　　C) Yes, certainly.

　　　　　　　D) That's interesting.

From the question we learn that the speaker is asking the listener to leave a message. Therefore, C) Yes, certainly is the correct answer. You should mark C) on the Answer Sheet. Now the test will begin.

1. A) She wants to play tennis.
   B) She likes to play tennis, but she doesn't want to play now.
   C) She always likes to play tennis.
   D) She does not like to play tennis.

2. A) He arrived at 5:20.　　　　　B) It was 4:25 when we met.
   C) I met him at 4:35.　　　　　D) We met at 5:05.

3. A) I had an accident.　　　　　B) I didn't go to work.
   C) I met an old friend.　　　　D) I don't believe in work.

4. A) It was late, so we didn't call you.
   B) It was not late until we called you.
   C) It was late, but we called you.
   D) It was late, but we didn't call you.

5. A) The driver asked John to get off the bus.
   B) John aksed the driver to let him off at the corner.

C) There is a bus stop near John's house.

D) John was a very careful bus driver.

Section B

Directions: This section is to test your ability to understand short conversations. There are 2 recorded conversations in it. After each conversation, there are some recorded questions. Both the conversations and questions will be spoken two times. When you hear a question, you should decide on the correct answer from the 4 choices marked A), B), C) and D) given in your test paper. Then you should mark the corresponding letter on the Answer Sheet with a single line through the centre.

Conversation 1

6. A) A performance.   B) A pop group.
   C) The name of a theatre.   D) The name of a dancer.
7. A) They are not going to the performance.
   B) The man will see the performance alone.
   C) They are going to see the performance together.
   D) The woman will see the performance alone.

Conversation 2

8. A) Tokyo.   B) New York.   C) Beijing.   D) Hong Kong.
9. A) He'll pay by credit card.   B) It'll be collected by himself.
   C) He'll pay by check.   D) It'll be delivered to him.
10. A) 5%.   B) 10%.   C) 15%.   D) 20%.

Section C

Directions: This section is to test your ability to comprehend short passages. You will hear a recorded passage. After that you will hear five questions. Both the passage and the questions will be read two times. When you hear a question, you should complete the answer to it with a word or a short phrase (in no more than 3 words). The incomplete answers are printed on your test paper. You should write your answers on the Answer Sheet correspondingly. Now the passages will begin.

11. How long did the speaker stay in Hollywood last Christmas?

    He stayed there for _____.

12. Where did the speaker meet his best friend?

    He met her at _____.

13. Why was the speaker disappointed when they drove to Hollywood?

    Because the place looked rather _____.

14. Where was the speaker's friend's house?

    It was located up in the _____.

15. How much time did they spend in Disneyland?

　　They spent there _____.

Part II Structure (15 minutes)

Directions: This part is to test your ability to construct grammatically correct sentences. It consists of 2 sections.

Section A

Directions: In this section, there are 10 incomplete sentences. You are required to complete each one by deciding on the most appropriate word or words from the 4 choices marked A), B), C) and D). Then you should mark the corresponding letter on the Answer Sheet with a single line through the centre.

16. As a matter of fact, they would rather leave for Beijing than _____ in Shanghai.

　　A) stay　　　　　　B) staying　　　　　　C) stayed　　　　　　D) to stay

17. It was not until yesterday evening _____ the manager made his decision known.

　　A) when　　　　　　B) that　　　　　　C) as　　　　　　D) so

18. I broke a dish while washing up this morning. Of course, I did not _____.

　　A) love to　　　　　　B) need to　　　　　　C) mean to　　　　　　D) want to

19. _____ is often the case, one third of the workers have over-fulfilled the production plan.

　　A) What　　　　　　B) This　　　　　　C) That　　　　　　D) As

20. We didn't finish the work in time. You _____ us since you were there.

　　A) might help

　　C) could have helped

　　B) should help

　　D) must have helped

21. Mr. Jones, _____ life was once very hard, is now very successful in his business.

　　A) of him　　　　　　B) his　　　　　　C) whose　　　　　　D) by whom

22. I decide to leave the company next month, where I _____ for exactly three years.

　　A) work

　　C) will be working

　　B) is working

　　D) have worked

23. The weather report says that there will be a storm _____ two days.

　　A) until　　　　　　B) before　　　　　　C) in　　　　　　D) by

24. Mary did not attend the meeting. _____.

　　A) Jane did too

　　C) So did Jane

　　B) Jane didn't as well

　　D) Nor did Jane

25. The May Day Holiday _____ over, we must now get down to work.

　　A) be　　　　　　B) being　　　　　　C) to have been　　　　　　D) to be

Section B

Directions: There are 10 incomplete statements here. You should fill in each blank with the proper form of the word given in the brackets. Write the word or words in the corresponding space on the Answer Sheet.

26. Last night we all went to the cinema, because the film was very (excite) _____.
27. My secretary asked me if I had anything else for her (type) _____ before she left.
28. This piece of music was composed by a very famous blind (music) _____.
29. If we (know) _____ that the books were available, we would have bought them yesterday.
30. Ms. Davis is proud of her students because they are not only (hard-work) _____, but also very creative.
31. The project was not actually realized as it was not very (practice) _____.
32. We were shocked to find that the man (come) _____ towards us was carrying a gun.
33. The Chairman of the Board explained his point again so that there would be no (understanding) _____.
34. We formally invited the General Manager of the Panda Group (attend) _____ our opening ceremony.
35. Tom took no notice of what I was saying because he thought I (cheat) _____ him.

Part III Reading Comprehension (40 minutes)

Directions: This part is to test your reading ability. There are 5 tasks for you to fulfil. You should read the reading materials carefully and do the tasks as you are instructed.

Task 1

Directions: After reading the following passage, you will find 5 questions or unfinished statements, numbered 36 through 40. For each question or statement there are 4 choices marked A), B), C) and D). You should make the correct choice and mark the corresponding letter on the Answer Sheet with a single line through the centre.

"But I just paid $1.69 for this bottle of wine last week. How come the price is now $2.25? What's going on?"

There are at least three things going on that have caused the price of wine to rise. All have to do with the supply and demand factors of economics.

The first factor is that people drinking more wine than ever before. This demand for more wine has increased overall (总体) wine sales in America at the rate of 15 percent a year.

The second factor is that the supply of wine has stayed relatively the same, which means that the same number of bottles is produced each year. Wine producers are trying to open up new land to grow more grapes (葡萄). But in at least three wine producing areas of the world — France, Germany, and California — new vineyards (葡萄园) will not be available in the near future. Wines are produced in other countries, such as Italy, Spain and Australia, but none of these countries will be able to fill the demand for good wines.

The third factor is that costs of wine production are increasing. The men who make wine are asking for more money, and the machinery needed to press the grapes is becoming more expensive.

When the demand for something is greater than the supply, prices go up. When production costs, meaning the price of labor and machinery, rise, the producer adds this increase to the price of the wine.

36. From the first paragraph, we know that the speaker is _____.
    A) asking about the price
    B) worrying about the price
    C) bargaining over the price
    D) complaining about the price

37. The three factors mentioned in the passage cause _____.
    A) the sales of wine to increase
    B) the price of wine to go up
    C) the production of wine to decrease
    D) more and more people to drink wine

38. The supply of wine has remained the same partly because _____.
    A) wine producing countries are unwilling to increase their production
    B) new vineyards will not be opened up in such countries as Australia
    C) countries like Italy and Spain can't supply enough good wines
    D) the production of wine bottles has ceased to increase

39. What does "production costs" refer to in the last paragraph?
    A) The price of grapes and machines.
    B) The cost of land and transportation.
    C) The price of wine and wine bottles.
    D) The cost of manpower and equipment.

40. The author's purpose of writing this passage is to _____.
    A) persuade people to drink less wine
    B) tell people where to get the best wine
    C) explain why the price of wine is rising
    D) show that wine is popular with Americans

Task 2

Directions: This task is the same as Task 1. The 5 questions or unfinished statements are numbered 41 through 45.

Airline companies are responsible for transporting your luggage. If you cannot recover it at the point of arrival, you must inform the airline immediately. They will carry out the necessary search. If the luggage is recovered, it will be delivered to your place of residence. If you wish to insure your luggage, you may do so at your own expense.

Some airlines restrict luggage weight to 44 pounds (20 kg); in other cases, there is no weight restriction, but you are not allowed more than two pieces of luggage. Inquire about luggage allowances from the airline with which you will be traveling. However, you must pay extra for excess luggage, which is not reimbursed (补偿) by Canadian International Development Agency (CIDA).

Each suitcase, bag or package must be clearly labeled with your name and destination. If you do not know the exact destination address at the time of your departure, label your luggage in care of (由……代收) the executing agency whose name appears in the Training Agreement, using the following model:

Surname, first name
Name of your country
Address of the executing agency
City, country, postal code
Telephone number of executing agency

If you do not have this information, please label your luggage with the name and address of the institution you are to attend in Canada. If none of these details are available, you can use CIDA's address.

41. If you can't find your luggage at the point of arrival, airline companies _____.
   A) ask you to insure your luggage
   B) deliver it to where you live
   C) inform you about its recovery
   D) ask you to pay some money for it

42. Before taking your air trip, you have to make sure _____.
   A) of the restrictions on luggage
   B) of the insurance for luggage
   C) who will pay for the excess luggage
   D) how much CIDA will pay for the excess luggage

43. The charge for the excess luggage should be paid by _____.
   A) CIDA
   B) the passenger
   C) the insurance company
   D) the executing agency

44. In case you have no idea at all where to send your luggage, you can send it to the address of _____.
   A) the institution you are to attend
   B) the airline you travel with
   C) the Canadian International Development Agency
   D) the executive agency given in the Training Agreement

45. The passage is mainly about CIDA's advice on _____.
   A) the charge of your luggage
   B) the handling of your luggage
   C) the insurance of your luggage

D) the transportation of your luggage

Task 3

Directions: The following is an advertisement. After reading it, you are required to complete the outline below it (numbered 46 through 50). You should write your answers briefly (in no more than 3 words) on the Answer Sheet correspondingly.

In order to meet readers' increasing demand for the latest information in the fast growing electronics and telecommunications industries, *China Daily* has formally launched publication of its IT (Information Technology) Page. Published every Sunday on Page 6 of Business Weekly in broadsheet format, the IT Page will keep you informed of the latest developments in the IT industry.

With *China Daily*'s quick, accurate, authoritative (权威的) and detailed reporting, the IT Page will, from a unique view, report and comment on the market trends, technological breakthroughs (突破) and industrial policies of the domestic and international computer, network, and telecommunications industries. Some special features such as interviews with experts, new product reviews, software listings, market researches and technical articles will also add to the interest and value of this page.

We welcome your submissions (preferably in English) and we hope IT companies will take advantage of our page to advertise their products and services.

Name of the Column: (46) _____.
Time of Publishing: (47) _____.
Contents: market trends, (48) _____ and industrial policies.
Purpose of the Column: to meet the readers' interest in the (49) _____ in the IT industry.
Advertisements Welcomed: from (50) _____.

Task 4

Directions: The following is a part of the contents of a computer handbook. After reading it, you are required to find the items equivalent (与……相同的) to those given in Chinese in the table below. Then you should put the corresponding letters in the brackets on the Answer Sheet, numbered 51 through 55.

A — Windows 98 at a Glance
B — Resources Included with Windows 98
C — Additional Resources
D — Running Windows 98 Setup
E — Selecting Setup Options
F — Logging on to Windows 98
G — Exploring Your Computer
H — Network Neighborhood
I — Working with Programs
J — Managing Files and Folders

K — Choosing a Desktop Style
L — Choosing Custom Settings
M — Delivering Web Control to Your Desktop
N — Using Multiple Monitors
O — Connecting to the Internet

Example：（O）连接 Internet （F）登录到 Windows 98

51. （　　）选择自定义设置
52. （　　）浏览计算机
53. （　　）其他资源
54. （　　）使用多功能监视器
55. （　　）网上邻居

Task 5

Directions：There is an advertisement below. After reading it you should give brief answers to the 5 questions (numbered. 56 through 60) that follow. The answers (in no more than 3 words) should be written after the corresponding numbers on the Answer Sheet.

7th July, 2001

Dear Sirs,

　　Headquartered in Chicago, Illinois, FMC Company is a major producer of technically advanced machinery and chemicals for industry and agriculture.

　　With a history dating back to 1884, FMC has grown to become one of the 100 largest industrial companies in the United States, with 2000's sales in excess of ＄2 billion. All over the world, FMC has about 41 600 employees at 129 factories in 32 states and 13 foreign countries.

　　We believe FMC to be one of the leaders of the packaging industry both in the U. S. and abroad. Through our own research, development and engineering efforts, we believe we are able to exchange views on and discuss the latest technical aspects of the industry.

　　FMC's packaging expertise (专长) is mainly in the following areas：

　　—Packaging and paper box making machinery；

　　—Wrapping machines for varying uses.

　　In the spirit of friendship, equality and mutual benefit, we look to a continued strengthening of our relationship with P. R. of China.

Faithfully yours,
FMC Co. Ltd.
General Manager

56. What does the company want to sell? _____.
57. Where is the Head Office of the company? In _____.
58. When did the company's annual sales exceed ＄2 billion? In the year of _____.
59. What role does the company think it plays in the world's packaging industry? _____.
60. To whom is the letter written? The letter is intended for _____ in P. R. of China.

Part IV Translation — English to Chinese（25 minutes）

Directions：This part, numbered 61 through 65, is to test your ability to translate English into Chinese. After each of the sentences numbered 61 to 64, you will read four choices of suggested translation. You should choose the best translation and mark the corresponding letter on the Answer Sheet. And for the paragraph numbered 65, write your translation in the corresponding space on the Translation/Composition Sheet.

61. Studies alone can conduct us to that enjoyment which is best in quality and infinite in quantity.
    A）单独学习能传达我们所喜欢的质量最好和数量无限的东西。
    B）学习能把我们带到高尚的、永无休止的娱乐之中。
    C）学习本身就能把我们带到至高无上的、无穷无尽的欢乐境地。
    D）全身心地学习会使我们在精神上得到激情和无限快乐。

62. The beauty of the scenery in our hometown passes all power of description.
    A）我们家乡风景之美，非言语所能形容。
    B）经过充分描述，我们家乡的风景更加美丽。
    C）我们家乡美丽的风景已超出了想象力。
    D）我们家乡以其所有的魅力显示她的美丽。

63. We appreciate the good quality of your products, but unfortunately your prices appear to be on the high side.
    A）我们很欣赏贵方产品的良好质量，不过遗憾的是贵方价格似乎太高了。
    B）我们很高兴贵厂的产品质量良好，只是贵方价格相当高。
    C）我们感谢你们提供的良好产品，但是你们的价格高得不当。
    D）我们感谢你们有良好的产品，可是你们提出的高价是不可取的。

64. If something urgent happens that prevents you from keeping the appointment, you can change or cancel the appointment immediately.
    A）假如有妨碍你约会的要紧事出现，你最好做出更改或取消约会的抉择。
    B）如果某事突发，使你不能如期约会，你应迅速对改变或取消约会做出反应。
    C）假如有急事需你另行约会，你可改变时间或及时进行约会。
    D）如果你有急事不能按时赴约，可以立即改变或取消约会。

65. On my return to the office this morning after being away for a few days, I found your kind invitation of the 1st October awaiting me, for which I thank you. I should like to have been in a position to accept your invitation, but unfortunately due to a prior engagement with some overseas friends, it will not be possible to do so.

Part V Writing（25 minutes）

Directions：This part is to test your ability to do practical writing. You are required to write a letter of complaint according to the information given in Chinese below. Remember to write the letter on the Translation/Composition Sheet.

说明：请以李玲女士的名义写一封投诉信。

李玲女士给某商店经理写信投诉该店的营业员服务质量差。昨天她赶上一场大雨，正巧路过此店，便进入此店到卖戒指的柜台，要求看一枚戒指，但 2 号营业员服务态度非常不好，拒绝提供服务。

时间：2010 年 6 月 20 日

Words for Reference：戒指 ring

Appendix　Glossary

A

abstract	[ˈæbstrækt]	n.	a short written statement containing the most important ideas in a speech, article etc. 摘要
account	[əˈkaunt]	n.	arrangement in which a bank keeps your money safe so that you can pay more in or take money out 账，账户
accustomed	[əˈkʌstəmd]	adj.	familiar with something and accepting it as normal or usual 习惯于
addiction	[əˈdikʃən]	n.	the state of being addicted or a habit to which one is addicted 上瘾，入迷
additional	[əˈdiʃənl]	adj.	more than what was agreed or expected 附加的，另外的
adjust	[əˈdʒʌst]	v.	to gradually become familiar with a new situation 调整，适应
advance	[ədˈvɑːns]	v.	to go or move (something) forward, or to develop or improve (something) 前进，增长
advantage	[ədˈvɑːntidʒ]	n.	the quality of having a superior or more favorable position 好处
affect	[əˈfekt]	v.	to have an effect upon 影响
agent	[ˈeidʒənt]	n.	a representative who acts on behalf of other persons or organizations; a person who works for a government or police department, especially in order to get secret information about another country or organization 代理人；特工
alcohol	[ˈælkəhɔl]	n.	drinks such as beer or wine that contain a substance which can make you drunk 酒，酒精
alternate	[ɔːlˈtəːnit]	adj.	(of sets of two) every second, or every other 交替的，轮流的，间隔的
	[ˈɔːltəːneit]	v.	to cause (two things) to happen or exist one after the other repeatedly 交替，轮流
amazing	[əˈmeiziŋ]	adj.	very surprising and causing pleasure or admiration 令人惊奇的
analyze	[ˈænəlaiz]	v.	to examine or think about something carefully, in order to understand it 分析，解析
animated	[ˈæniˌmeitid]	adj.	producing in the form of cartons (影片等)以动画形式制作的
appeal	[əˈpiːl]	n.	attractiveness that interests, pleases somebody or stimulates 吸引力
argue	[ˈɑːgjuː]	v.	to present reasons and arguments 争论，辩论，认为
argument	[ˈɑːgjumənt]	n.	a fact or assertion offered as evidence that something is true 论据
arouse	[əˈrauz]	v.	to call forth (emotions, feelings, and responses) 引起
aspect	[ˈæspekt]	n.	a distinct feature or element in a problem 方面
assessment	[əˈsesmənt]	n.	the act of judging or assessing 估计，评估
assignment	[əˈsainmənt]	n.	a duty that you are assigned to perform (分派的)工作，任务
astronaut	[ˈæstrɔːnɔːt]	n.	a person trained to travel in a spacecraft 宇航员

athlete	[ˈæθliːt]	n.	a person trained to compete in sports 运动员
attitude	[ˈætitjuːd]	n.	a complex mental state involving beliefs, feelings, values and dispositions to act in certain ways 态度
available	[əˈveiləb(ə)l]	adj.	obtainable or accessible and ready for use or service 可用的；可得到的
available	[əˈveiəbl]	adj.	ready for use or service 可用的，可得到的，有用的
award	[əˈwɔːd]	n.	something given for victory or superiority in a contest or competition or for winning a lottery 奖，奖品

B

back	[bæk]	v.	to give support or one's approval to somebody or something 支持
backlash	[ˈbæklæʃ]	n.	a strong negative reaction by a large number of people 强烈抵制，集体反对
benefit	[ˈbenifit]	n.	a helpful or good effect 利益
		v.	to be useful or profitable to 有益于；得益
bleed	[bliːd]	v.	to lose blood from one's body 流血
bless	[bles]	v.	to ask God to protect someone or something 保佑，祝福
bloom	[bluːm]	v.	to be in a healthy growing state; flourish 兴旺，繁盛
bond	[bɔnd]	n.	something that unites two or more people or groups, such as love, or a shared interest or idea 联系，关系
bonus	[ˈbəunəs]	n.	an extra amount of money given to someone as a reward for work or as encouragement 红利，奖金
bore	[bɔː]	v.	to cause to be bored 使厌烦
budget	[ˈbʌdʒit]	n.	the money that is available to an organization or person, or a plan of how it will be spent 预算
buzzword	[ˈbʌzwəːd]	n.	a word or phrase related to a particular subject, that has become fashionable and popular and is used a lot in newspapers 时髦词语，漂亮口号

C

cancel	[ˈkænsl]	v.	to call off; to postpone 取消，撤销
capability	[ˌkeipəˈbiləti]	n.	the natural ability, skill, or power 能力，才能，性能
capri pants			卡普里裤，七分裤
cardboard	[ˈkɑːdbɔːd]	n.	a stiff moderately thick paper 厚纸板
career	[kəˈriə]	n.	job 职业，事业
case	[keis]	n.	a problem requiring investigation 案件
casual	[ˈkæʒjuəl]	adj.	not formal 非正式的，随便的
casually	[ˈkæʒjuəli]	adv.	not methodically or according to plan 任意地，随便地，胡乱地
celebrate	[ˈselibreit]	v.	to observe (a birthday, anniversary, etc.) 庆祝，祝贺
cereal	[ˈsiəriəl]	n.	a plant grown to produce grain, for example, wheat, rice etc. 谷类食物
challenge	[ˈtʃælindʒ]	n.	something that tests strength, skill, or ability, especially in a way

Appendix

			that is interesting 挑战
challenge	[ˈtʃælindʒ]	v.	to issue a challenge to 向……挑战
character	[ˈkæriktə]	n.	an imaginary person represented in a work of fiction (play/film/story) 人物
character	[ˈkæriktə(r)]	n.	the mental and moral qualities distinctive to an individual 性格
charity	[ˈtʃæriti]	n.	an organization that gives money, goods, or help to people who are poor, sick etc. 慈善，慈善机构
church	[tʃɜːtʃ]	n.	a place for public (especially Christian) worship 教堂
cite	[sait]	vt.	to mention something as an example, especially one that supports, proves, or explains an idea or situation 引用，引证
club	[klʌb]	n.	a formal association of people with similar interests 社团，俱乐部
code	[kəud]	v.	to convert ordinary language into code 写成密码或代码
comfort	[ˈkʌmfət]	n.	a state of being relaxed and feeling no pain 舒适，安慰
comic	[ˈkɔmik]	n.	a book or magazine containing comic strips 连环漫画，连环画册
comment	[ˈkɔment]	v.	to express an opinion about someone or something 评论
committee	[kəˈmiti]	n.	a special group delegated to consider some matter 委员会
communicate	[kəˈmjuːnikeit]	v.	to transmit information 交流
communication	[kəˌmjuːniˈkeiʃən]	n.	the process by which people exchange information or express their thoughts and feelings 沟通，交通，信息
compare	[kəmˈpɛə(r)]	v.	to examine and note the similarities or differences of two or more people or things 比较
complain	[kəmˈplein]	v.	to express complaints, discontent, displeasure, or unhappiness 抱怨
composer	[kəmˈpəuzə]	n.	a person who composes music 创作者（尤指乐曲）
concern	[kənˈsəːn]	n.	something that interests you because it is important or affects you 关心，忧虑，关心的事
		v.	have to do with or be relevant to 涉及，影响，关心
conduct	[kənˈdʌkt]	v.	to organize and direct (a particular activity) 实施
confirm	[kənˈfəːm]	v.	to show that something is definitely true, especially by providing more proof 证实
conflict	[ˈkɔnflikt]	n.	a state of opposition between persons, ideas or interests 矛盾，抵触，不一致
constant	[ˈkɔnstənt]	adj.	happening regularly or all the time 经常的，不变的
contact	[ˈkɔntækt]	n.	communication with a person, organization, country etc. 联系，联络，交往
contribute	[kənˈtribjuːt]	v.	to give something (especially money) in order to help achieve or provide something 有助于
convenient	[kənˈviːnjənt]	adj.	suited to your comfort, purpose or needs 方便的
correlated	[ˈkɔːrəˌleitid]	adj.	mutually related 相互关联的
correspond	[ˌkɔrisˈpɔnd]	v.	to exchange messages or letters 通信，联络
counseling	[ˈkaunsəliŋ]	n.	the job or process of listening to someone and giving them advice about their problems 咨询服务
counter	[ˈkauntə]	v.	to react (to something) with an opposing opinion or action 反对，

161

			反击
count	[kaunt]	v.	to consider somebody/something in a particular way; to calculate 认为，视为；计算
creator	[kri'eitə]	n.	a person who creates; originator 创造者，创作者
credit card			a small plastic card that you use to buy goods or services and pay for them later 信用卡
criticize	['kritisaiz]	v.	to express your disapproval of someone or something, or to talk about their faults 批评
crucifixion	[ˌkruːsi'fikʃən]	n.	the death of Jesus on the cross 耶稣被钉死在十字架上
cruise	[kruːz]	n.	an ocean trip taken for pleasure 巡游，巡航
cryptologist	[krip'tɔlədʒist]	n.	the person who studies the science of analysing or deciphering codes 密码学家
curious	['kjuəriəs]	adj.	eagerly interested in learning more 好奇的
current	['kʌrənt]	adj.	belonging to the present time 现在的，当前的
cute	[kjuːt]	adj.	lovely 可爱的，聪明的
cyberspace	['saibəspeis]	n.	a computer network consisting of a worldwide network 网络空间

D

decade	['dekeid]	n.	a period of ten years 十年
definitely	['definitli]	adv.	without question and beyond doubt 明确地，确切地
delete	[di'liːt]	v.	to remove; to wipe out 删除
demonstrate	['demənstreit]	v.	to show or prove something clearly 示范，演示，证明
dependency	[di'pendənsi]	n.	a state of needing something or someone, especially in order to continue existing or operating 依赖，从属
depression	[di'preʃən]	n.	a medical condition that makes you very unhappy and anxious 沮丧，抑郁
desert	[di'zəːt]	v.	to leave someone or something, and no longer help or support them 遗弃
design	[di'zain]	v.	to make a drawing or plan of something that will be made or built 计划，设计
detail	['diːteil]	v.	to list things or give all the facts or information about something 详述
		n.	a particular fact or item of information 细节，详情
digital	['didʒitl]	adj.	recording or showing information in the form of numbers 数字的，数码的
disadvantage	[disəd'vɑːntidʒ]	n.	something that causes problems, or that makes someone or something less likely to be successful or effective 不利，不利条件
disadvantage	[ˌdisəd'vɑːntidʒ]	n.	the quality of having an inferior or less favorable position 不利
disclose	[dis'kləuz]	vt.	to make something publicly known 揭露
discount	['diskaunt]	n.	a reduction in the usual price of something 折扣
doll	[dɔl]	n.	toy 玩偶，（玩具）娃娃
download	['daunləud]	vt.	to move information or programs from a computer network to a small

			computer 下载
dressy	[ˈdresi]	adj.	in fancy clothing 衣着华丽的
due	[djuː]	adj.	scheduled to arrive, suitable to or expected in the circumstances 到期的，应有的；适当的，正当的

E

edit	[ˈedit]	v.	to prepare a book, piece of film etc. for printing or broadcasting by removing mistakes or parts that are not acceptable 编辑，编校，修订
efficient	[iˈfiʃənt]	adj.	being effective without wasting time or effort 效率高的，胜任的
emerge	[iˈməːdʒ]	v.	to come out of a dark, confined or hidden place 出现，浮现
employee	[ˌemplɔiˈiː]	n.	a person who is paid to work for someone else 雇员
encounter	[inˈkauntə]	n.	a meeting, especially one that is unplanned or unexpected 碰见，偶然相遇
encourage	[inˈkʌridʒ]	vt.	to give hope or courage to somebody 鼓励，鼓舞
endure	[inˈdjuə]	v.	to put up with something or somebody unpleasant 忍耐，容忍
engage	[inˈgeidʒ]	v.	to agree to marry 订婚
engagement	[inˈgeidʒmənt]	n.	a mutual promise to marry 订婚
ensure	[inˈʃuə]	v.	to make certain that an event or activity will happen properly 保证，确保
essence	[ˈesns]	n.	the most basic and important quality of something 精髓
estimate	[ˈestimeit]	n.	an approximate calculation of quantity, degree or worth 估计
evidence	[ˈevidəns]	n.	basis for belief or disbelief; knowledge on which to base belief 根据，证据
exaggerated	[igˈzædʒəreitid]	adj.	enlarged to an abnormal degree 夸张的，夸大的
excel	[ikˈsel]	v.	to distinguish oneself 超过，优于
exchange	[iksˈtʃeindʒ]	v.	to give and receive (information, ideas, etc) 交换
executive	[igˈzekjutiv]	n.	a person or a group of people responsible for the administration of a company or an organization 执行者，主管；行政部门
expand	[iksˈpænd]	v.	to become larger in size, number, or amount 增加，扩展，使……膨胀
expert	[ˈekspəːt]	n.	a person with special knowledge or ability who performs skillfully 专家，能手
extract	[iksˈtrækt]	v.	to remove (used in an abstract sense) 选取，摘录

F

Facebook	[ˈfeisbuk]	n.	脸谱网（美国的一个社交网站）
faculty	[ˈfækəlti]	n.	the body of teachers at a school 全体教员
failing	[ˈfeiliŋ]	n.	a flaw or weak point 失败，缺点，过失
fascinate	[ˈfæsineit]	v.	to cause to be interested or curious 使着迷
feedback	[ˈfiːdbæk]	n.	advice, criticism or information about how good or useful something or somebody's work is 反馈

female	[ˈfiːmeil]	adj.	being a woman or a girl 雌的，女（性）的
fiancé	[fiˈɑːnsei]	n.	〈法〉未婚夫（fiancée 未婚妻）
financial	[faiˈnænʃəl]	adj.	relating to money or the management of money 金融的，财政的
firefighter	[ˈfaiəˌfaitə]	n.	a member of a fire department who tries to extinguish fires 消防队员
fireplace	[ˈfaiəpleis]	n.	an open space for a fire in the wall of a room 壁炉
flexibility	[ˌfleksəˈbiliti]	n.	ability to change to suit different needs or situations 灵活性
flip-flop	[ˈflipflɔp]	n.	夹趾拖鞋
Florida	[ˈflɔridə]	n.	佛罗里达（美国的一个州）
focus	[ˈfəukəs]	v.	to direct one's attention on something （使）集中，聚集
formality	[fɔːˈmæliti]	n.	something that you must do as a formal or official part of an activity or process 礼节，程序
format	[ˈfɔːmæt]	n.	the general appearance of a publication 格式
frequency	[ˈfriːkwənsi]	n.	the number of times that something happens within a particular period of time or within a particular group of people 频繁
furniture	[ˈfəːnitʃə]	n.	objects that can be moved, such as tables, chairs and beds, that are put into a house or an office to make it suitable for living or working in 家具

G

gambling	[ˈgæmbliŋ]	n.	activities in which people risk money or possessions on the result of something which is not certain, such as a card game or a horse race 赌博，投机
garage	[ˈgærɑːʒ]	n.	a building for keeping the car in, usually next to or attached to a house 车库
generation	[ˌdʒenəˈreiʃən]	n.	all the people living at the same time or of about the same age 代，一代
geographical	[ˌdʒiːəˈgræfikl]	adj.	of or relating to the science of geography 地理的，地理学的
grail	[greil]	n.	（通常作 the Holy Grail）plate or cup used by Jesus 圣杯
grocery (store)	[ˈgrəusəri]	n.	a store where food and small items for the house are sold 食品杂货店
guideline	[ˈgaidlain]	n.	rules or instructions about the best way to do something 指引，指导方针

H

handle	[ˈhænd(ə)l]	v.	to manage (a situation or problem) 处理
harmonious	[hɑːˈməuniəs]	adj.	existing together in harmony 和谐的
heartening	[ˈhɑːtniŋ]	adj.	making you feel happier and more positive 振奋人心的
Hildebrandt	[ˈhildəbrænt]	n.	希尔德布兰德（人名）
holy	[ˈhəuli]	adj.	associated with a divine power 神圣的，圣洁的
honor	[ˈɔnə]	v.	to show respect towards somebody 尊敬
horizon	[həˈraizn]	n.	the limit of your ideas, knowledge, and

			experience 视野，眼界
humor	[ˈhjuːmə]	n.	the quality of being funny 幽默，诙谐

I

ID	[ˌaiˈdiː]	n.	a document that shows one's name and date of birth, usually with a photograph (=identification) 身份证
immediate	[iˈmiːdiət]	adj.	happening or done at once and without delay 立即的，直接的
immerse	[iˈməːs]	v.	to become or make somebody completely involved in something 沉浸在……
inconsistent	[ˌinkənˈsistənt]	adj.	lack of consistency or agreement 不一致的
independent	[ˌindiˈpendənt]	adj.	not influenced or controlled by other people and free to make your own decisions 独立的，自主的
individual	[ˌindiˈvidjuəl]	n.	a person, considered separately from the rest of the group or society that they live in 个人，个体
individuality	[ˌindiˌvidʒuˈæləti]	n.	the qualities that make someone or something different from other things or people 个性，人格，特征
information	[ˌinfəˈmeiʃən]	n.	facts or details that tell you something about a situation, person, event etc. 信息，情报，新闻，资料
information	[ˌinfə(r)ˈmeiʃ(ə)n]	n.	a message received and understood 信息
initial	[iˈniʃəl]	adj.	occurring at the beginning 开始的，最初的
initially	[iˈniʃəli]	adv.	at the beginning 起初，最初
inner	[ˈinə(r)]	adj.	located or occurring within or closer to a center 内在的
innocent	[ˈinəsnt]	adj.	free from evil or guilt 无罪的
inspiration	[ˌinspəˈreiʃən]	n.	a person or thing that stimulates in this way 鼓舞人心的人或事物
inspire	[inˈspaiə]	v.	to give somebody the idea for something, especially something artistic or that shows imagination 赋予灵感，引起联想
instant	[ˈinstənt]	adj.	happening immediately 立即的，即时的
		n.	a very short moment of time, or a particular point in time 立即，瞬间
intellectual	[ˌintiˈlektʃuəl]	adj.	of or relating to the intellect 智力
interval	[ˈintəvəl]	n.	a period of time between two events 间隔，间歇

J

journal	[ˈdʒəːnl]	n.	a newspaper or magazine that deals with a particular subject of profession; a daily written record of experiences; diary 杂志，期刊，报纸，日报，日记

K

Kelly	[ˈkeli]	n.	凯莉（人名）
knowledge	[ˈnɔlidʒ]	n.	facts, information, and skills acquired by a person through experience or education 知识

L

lack	[læk]	v.	to be without 缺乏，不足
limited	[ˈlimitid]	adj.	small in range or scope 有限的
line	[lain]	n.	text consisting of a row of words written across a page or computer screen（诗文的）一行
live	[laiv]	adj.	actually being performed at the time of hearing or viewing 直播的
loyalty	[ˈlɔiəlti]	n.	the quality of being faithful in your support of somebody or something 忠诚，忠实

M

magnificent	[mægˈnifis(ə)nt]	adj.	impressively beautiful, elaborate, or extravagant; striking 壮丽的，宏伟的
maintain	[meinˈtein]	v.	to keep in a certain state, position, or activity 维持
makeup	[ˈmeikʌp]	n.	colored substances that are put on your face to improve or change your appearance 化妆品
mantle	[ˈmæntl]	n.	shelf that projects from wall above fireplace 壁炉台架
match	[mætʃ]	n.	one that is like another in one or more specified qualities 相配，般配的人或事物
maximum	[ˈmæksiməm]	adj.	being the largest amount or number allowed or possible 最高的，最大极限的
merely	[ˈmiəli]	adv.	and nothing more 仅仅，只不过
metaphor	[ˈmetəfə]	n.	use of a word or phrase to indicate something different 隐喻
mistrust	[misˈtrʌst]	v.	to have doubts or suspicions about somebody or something 不信任
mock	[mɔk]	v.	to laugh at 嘲笑，嘲弄
multitask	[ˌmʌltiˈtæsk]	vt.	to work at several different tasks simultaneously（multitasker n.）使多任务化
murder	[ˈməːdə]	n.	unlawful killing of a human being 谋杀

N

namesake	[ˈneimseik]	n.	a person with the same name as another 同名人，同名物
negative	[ˈnegətiv]	adj.	having the quality of something harmful or unpleasant 否定的，负的，消极的
nervous	[ˈnəːvəs]	adj.	causing or fraught with or showing anxiety. 神经紧张的，不安的
network	[ˈnetwəːk]	n.	a group formed from parts that are connected together 网络，系统
novel	[ˈnɔvəl]	n.	a extended fictional work in prose, usually in the form of a story 小说

O

occasional	[əˈkeiʒənəl]	adj.	occurring from time to time 偶尔的，不时的
occupation	[ˌɔkjuˈpeiʃən]	n.	a job or profession 职业
opportunist	[ˈɔpətjuːnist]	n.	someone who uses every opportunity to gain power,

			money, or unfair advantages 机会主义者，投机者
oppose	[əˈpəuz]	v.	to disagree with something such as a plan or idea and try to prevent it from happening or succeeding 反对，反抗
option	[ˈɔpʃn]	n.	a choice you can make in a particular situation 选择（权），可选物
outline	[ˈautlain]	n.	a summary of the main points of an argument or theory 大纲，概要
overall	[əuvəˈrɔ:l]	adj.	including everything 全部的，全体的，一切在内的
overview	[ˈəuvəˌvju:]	n.	a general summary of a subject 概况，总结

P

pal	[pæl]	n.	a close friend 朋友，伙伴
participant	[pɑ:ˈtisipənt]	n.	someone who is taking part in an activity or event 参与者
passion	[ˈpæʃən]	n.	strong feeling or emotion 激情，热情
perfect	[ˈpə:(r)fikt]	adj.	being complete of its kind and without defect or blemish 完美的
personal	[ˈpə:sənəl]	adj.	of or relating to the private aspects of a person's life 个人的，私人的
PIN	[pin]		personal identification number 个人标识号
plot	[plɔt]	n.	the story that is told in a novel, play, movie etc. 故事情节
poorly-designed	[ˌpuəli-diˈzaind]	adj.	of something designed inadequately 设计不科学的
popular	[ˈpɔpjulə]	adj.	regarded with great favor, approval or affection, especially by the general public 大众的，流行的
poser	[ˈpəuzə]	n.	someone who pretends to have a quality or social position 装腔作势的人
positive	[ˈpɔzətiv]	adj.	having the quality of something good and pleasant 肯定的，积极的，正面的
postal	[ˈpəustəl]	adj.	of or relating to the system for delivering mail 邮政的
potential	[pəˈtenʃl]	adj.	likely to develop into a particular type of person or thing in the future 可能的，潜在的
		n.	the possibility that something will develop in a particular way, or have a particular effect 潜力，潜能
pregnant	[ˈpregnənt]	adj.	carrying offspring within the body or being about to produce new life 怀孕的
present	[priˈzent]	v.	to show or demonstrate something to an interested audience 展示，展现
previous	[ˈpri:vjəs]	adj.	happening or existing before the one mentioned 在……之前的，以前的
priority	[praiˈɔriti]	n.	status established in order of importance or urgency 优先权
professional	[prəˈfeʃənəl]	adj.	relating to a job that needs special education and training 专业的
proposal	[prəˈpəuzl]	n.	a plan or suggestion 提议，建议
prospective	[prəˈspektiv]	adj.	related to the future 未来的，预期的
provoke	[prəˈvəuk]	v.	to cause a particular reaction or have a particular effect 激起，引起，引发

publish	[ˈpʌblɪʃ]	v.	to make available to the public, usually by printing a book, magazine, newspaper, or other document 出版，发行
puzzle	[ˈpʌzl]	n.	question that is difficult to understand or answer 难题，谜一样的事物
		v.	to make somebody think hard, perplex 使困惑

Q

quality	[ˈkwɔliti]	n.	something that people may have as part of their character, for example, courage or intelligence 品质，特质

R

rate	[reit]	v.	to estimate the value or quality of somebody or something 估价，定等级
recall	[riˈkɔːl]	v.	to recollect knowledge from memory 回忆，回想
related	[riˈleitid]	adj.	be in a relationship with 相关的，有关系的，同种的
relevant	[ˈrelivənt]	adj.	having a connection with the subject at issue 相关的，切题的
relight	[ˌriːˈlait]	v.	to light again 重新点燃
remain	[riˈmein]	v.	to stay the same; to keep in a certain state 保持
renovation	[ˌrenəˈveiʃən]	n.	the act of improving by renewing and restoring 更新；修复
resentment	[riˈzentmənt]	n.	a feeling of deep and bitter anger and ill-will 怨恨，愤恨
resistance	[riˈzistəns]	n.	the action of opposing something 抵抗力，反抗
retire	[riˈtaiə]	n./v.	to stop performing one's work or withdraw from one's position 退休，退职
reunite	[ˌriːjuːˈnait]	v.	to have a reunion; to unite again 重聚，重新结合
reveal	[riˈviːl]	vt.	to make known something that was previously secret or unknown 显示，透露
rigid	[ˈridʒid]	adj.	very strict and difficult to change 刻板的，严格的
ruin	[ruin]	v.	to destroy or cause to fail 毁灭，毁坏

S

scandal	[ˈskændl]	n.	a disgraceful event 丑闻，丑行
schedule	[ˈskedʒul]	n.	a list of planned activities or things to be done at or during a particular time 时间表，一览表，计划
		vt.	to plan something for a particular time 安排，计划
search bar		n.	搜索栏
secure	[siˈkjuə]	adj.	free from danger or risk 安心的，安全的
self-centered	[ˌselfˈsentəd]	adj.	interested only in oneself 以自我为中心的
self-confidence	[selfˈkɔnfidəns]	n.	belief in yourself and your abilities 自信
self-fulfillment	[selfulˈfilmənt]	n.	the fulfillment of your capacities 自我实现
self-reported	[ˈselfriˈpɔːtid]	adj.	reported by oneself 自我报告的
sentimental	[ˌsentiˈmentl]	adj.	easily affected by emotions such as love, sympathy 感伤性的，感情脆弱的

Appendix

separation	[ˌsepəˈreiʃən]	n.	the act of dividing or disconnecting 分开，离开
ship	[ʃip]	v.	to transport by ship（用船）运送，装运，上（船）
shortcoming	[ˈʃɔː(r)tˌkʌmiŋ]	n.	a fault or failure to meet a certain standard, typically in a person's character, a plan, or a system 缺点
similarity	[ˌsimiˈlæriti]	n.	the quality of being similar 相似，类似
smart	[smɑːt]	adj.	characterized by quickness and ease in learning 聪明的
snail mail			the system of sending letters by post 蜗牛邮件（指通过邮局邮递的邮件）
society	[səˈsaiəti]	n.	an extended social group having a distinctive cultural and economic organization 社会
source	[sɔːs]	n.	something or somebody that causes or produces something, or is the origin of it 来源
specialist	[ˈspeʃəlist]	n.	someone who knows a lot about a particular subject, or is very skilled at it 专家
spit	[spit]	v.	to force something out of your mouth 吐，吐痰
spray	[sprei]	v.	to cover something with very small drops of a liquid that are forced out of a container or sent through the air 喷，喷洒
spread	[spred]	v.	to open from a closed or folded state 展开
stimulate	[ˈstimjuleit]	v.	to stir somebody's feelings, emotions, or peace 激励，鼓舞
straightforward	[streitˈfɔːwəd]	adj.	frank 坦率的，直接的
strategy	[ˈstrætidʒi]	n.	skillful planning in general 战略，策略
strip	[strip]	n.	a sequence of drawings telling a story in a newspaper or comic book 连环漫画
subdivision	[ˈsʌbdiˌviʒən]	n.	an area composed of subdivided lots 细分，再分的部分
subject	[ˈsʌbdʒikt]	n.	some situation or event that is thought about 主题，话题，题材
subsection	[ˈsʌbˌsekʃən]	n.	a section of a section 小单位，细分
suffer	[ˈsʌfə]	v.	to experience or show the effects of something bad 遭受，忍受
suggest	[səˈdʒest]	v.	to show (an idea or feeling) without stating it directly 暗示
			to mention (an idea, possible plan, or action) for other people to consider 提议，建议
summit	[ˈsʌmit]	n.	the highest stage of development 顶点，顶峰
supposition	[ˌsʌpəˈziʃən]	n.	a message expressing an opinion based on incomplete evidence 假设，推测，推想
surf	[səːf]	v.	to move quickly from one place to another on the Internet to learn what each place is offering 网上冲浪，浏览
surname	[ˈsəːneim]	n.	a name shared in common to identify the members of a family 姓
survey	[səːˈvei]	n.	a set of questions that you ask a large number of people in order to find out their opinions or behaviour 调查
	[səˈvei]	v.	to ask a large number of people questions in order to find out their attitudes or opinions 调查，审视
suspense	[səˈspens]	n.	eagerness about what is going to happen 悬疑，焦虑，悬念
symbology	[simˈbɔlədʒi]	n.	the study or the use of symbols or symbolism 符号学

symptom	[ˈsimptəm]	n.	any single problem which is caused by and shows a more serious and general problem 症状

T

tattoo	[tæˈtuː]	n.	a pattern or a picture put on the skin by tattooing 文身
temporarily	[ˈtempərərili]	adv.	for a limited time only 暂时地，临时地
Texas	[ˈteksəs]	n.	德克萨斯（美国的一个州）
thesis	[ˈθiːsis]	n.	a statement as a premise in an argument 论题，主题
three-dimensional	[ˌθriːdiˈmenʃənəl]	adj.	involving or relating to three dimensions or aspects 三维的，三度的，立体的，生动的
thriller	[ˈθrilə]	n.	a suspenseful adventure story 惊险小说
thrive	[θraiv]	v.	to grow stronger 兴旺，繁荣，茁壮成长
timing	[ˈtaimiŋ]	n.	the time when something happens 时机，时间的选择和安排
traffic	[ˈtræfik]	n.	pedestrians or vehicles coming and going 交通
treasure	[ˈtreʒə]	n.	a collection of precious things 珠宝，珍品
tribe	[traib]	n.	a group or class of people, especially of one profession 一伙人，一帮人

U

unreasonable	[ʌnˈriːz(ə)nəb(ə)l]	adj.	not guided by or based on good sense 不合理的
unusual	[ʌnˈjuːʒuəl]	adj.	out of the ordinary; uncommon; extraordinary 不平常的，异常的

V

verify	[ˈverifai]	v.	to make sure that a factor or an argument is true 查证，证实
violence	[ˈvaiələns]	n.	an act of aggression (as one against a person who resists) 暴力
vow	[vau]	v.	to promise solemnly 发誓，庄严地承诺

W

wedding	[ˈwediŋ]	n.	the ceremony or celebration of a marriage 婚礼
wheelchair	[ˈwiːlˌtʃɛə]	n.	a chair with wheels, used by people who cannot walk 轮椅
wifi	[ˈwaifai]	abbr.	(= Wireless Fidelity) n. [U] a system for connecting electronic equipment such as computers and electronic organizers to the Internet without using wires 无线局域网
witness	[ˈwitnis]	vt. &n.	to be present at or have personal knowledge of 出席，见证
wonder	[ˈwʌndə]	v.	to have a wish or desire to know something 想知道

Y

yearbook	[ˈjiəˌbuk]	n.	a book published once a year, giving details of events of the previous year 年鉴，年刊